DREAM-LIF

THIS BOOK is the first major revision of Freud's Theory of Dreams within the framework of the Structural Theory. It explores the structure and functions of dream life as a crucial aspect of the symbolic area of mental life, using the concepts of Melanie Klein, particularly the concreteness of psychic reality and the spacial structure of the world of the mind. Added to this background is Wilfred Bion's Theory of Thinking and Ernst Cassirer's Philosophy of Symbolic Forms as the theoretical basis for exploring the relation of dreams to thought processes, language usage and actions in the world. The implications of this Structural Theory for the practice of dream exploration and dream interpretation make up the second part of the book, placing this aspect of psycho-analytical technique and method on a new and firmer foundation.

Dream-Life

A Re-Examination of the Psychoanalytic Theory and Technique

Donald Meltzer

Published for
The Harris Meltzer Trust by

KARNAC

© The Roland Harris Educational Trust
First published 1984

This edition published in 2009 by
Karnac Books Ltd
118 Finchley Road, London NW3 5HT

Copyright © 2009 by The Harris Meltzer Trust
www.harris-meltzer-trust.org.uk

British Library Cataloguing in Publication Data
A C.I.P. for this book is available from the British Library

ISBN-13: 978-1-85575-619-9

www.karnacbooks.com

Contents

Acknowledgements

I wish to express my gratitude to the many people who have encouraged and assisted me in the preparation of this book.

First I must mention those who have been kind enough, and bold enough, to allow me to use their clinical material:

Dr Assunta Tondini of the Instituto Neuropsiciatria Infantile, Calambrone di Pisa

Mlle Cleo Athenasieu of Paris

Mr George Crawford, London

Mrs Marja Shulman, Helsinki

Mr Richard Emmanuel, London

Mrs Catharine Mack Smith, Oxford

Second, my thanks go to the two people who have helped most with the preparation of the manuscript:

Mrs Francesca Bion who read the typescript and the page proofs, and advised in many ways

Mrs Catharine Mack Smith who prepared the index and bibliography, and earlier had revised the literary style

Finally, I must mention with humble thanks the three people whose encouragement at every stage quickened my unwilling pace of composition:

Mrs Martha Harris

Mrs Margaret Williams

Mrs Morag Majo

Thy sweveness eek and al swich fantasye
Dryf out, and lat hem faren to mischaunce;
For they procede of thy meloncolye,
That doth thee fele in slepe al this penaunce..
A straw for alle swevenes significaunce!
God helpe me so, I counte hem not a bene,
Ther woot no man aright what dremes mene..

For prestes of the temple tellen this,
That dremes been the revelaciouns
Of goddes, and as wel they telle, y-wis,
That they ben infernals illusiouns;
And leches seyn, that of complexiouns
Proceden they, or fast, or glotonye.
Who woot in sooth thus what they signifye?

Eke othere seyn that thorugh impressiouns,
As if a wight hath faste a thing in minde,
That ther-of cometh swiche avisiouns;
And othere seyn, as they in bokes finde,
That, after tymes of the yeer by kinde,
Men dreme, and that th'effect goth by the mone;
But leve no dreme, for it is nought to done.

Wel worth of dremes ay thise old wyves,
And trweliche eek augurie of thise foules;
For fere of which men wenen lese her lyves,
As ravenes qualm, or shryking of thise oules.
To trowen on it bothe fals and foul is.
Allas, allas, so noble a creature
As is a man, shal drede swich ordure!

Chaucer: *Troilus and Criseyde, Book V*

PART A

THEORETICAL BACKGROUND

I

Freud's View of the Dream as the Guardian of Sleep

Unless it commences on a firm ground of Freud's pioneer work, no undertaking to examine dreams and dream-life from the psycho-analytical point of view can go any considerable distance into the problem without creating more confusion than clarity. But a truly critical, rather than merely appreciative, view of his accomplishment runs almost immediately into the problem, writ large in the early days of his psychological career, of a baffling division between his tendency to form and prove rigid theories, and his extraordinary capacity for observation and imaginative speculation.

Before we can proceed with an examination of the rich and fascinating array of observations and conjectures, it is necessary to state and examine the less interesting theory, mainly in order to set it aside in our future exposition. The brevity may seem dismissive, but this would be unjust. There cannot be the slightest doubt of the historical importance of the theory and the groundwork it laid for the evolution of clinical practice. And much can be salvaged that is enduringly interesting, such as the concepts of censorship and dream-work. But the basis of the theory is so deeply rooted in a neurophysiological model of the mind, with its mind-brain equation, that it will not bear the weight of investigations into the meaning of the meaning of dreams.

A. *The Guardian of Sleep* – none of the evidence that Freud brought to bear in this respect argues any more strongly for the thesis that dreams are the guardians of sleep than that they are its destroyers. The hypothesis was bound so completely to the assumption that sleep is a purely physiological process, that waking and sleeping stand in relation to the brain as catabolism and anabolism do to the body as a whole. No other purpose could possibly be assigned that would see dreams as valuable to the organism in the Darwinian sense.

Consequently Freud had only two choices: to view dreams as the protector or as the disturber of the physiological event. The same problem can be seen to have exercised physiologists in regard to physical pain. At a time prior to the discovery that pain is transmitted by particular fibres to particular centres of the central nervous system, it was quite natural to assume a quantitative basis for the differentiation of pleasurable and painful stimuli. And Freud adopted this same view in regard to mental pain. The whole model of the mind was unfavourable to the consideration of processes from a qualitative standpoint and Freud's wide experience in the neurophysiology laboratory disposed him naturally to a quantitative view. That it was the most respectable view in the medical profession could not have failed to move him, as so many of his own dreams in the *Traumdeutung* strongly confirm. But in the world of Romantic literature and art a very different view was equally respectable. In the world of the "romantic agony" characters were repeatedly being depicted as haunted by their dreams, fearful of sleep lest they be repeated.

B. *The Dream as Wish-fulfilment* – it is not possible to derive from Freud's writings any clear conception of what he means by "wish". Intention, motive, plan, desire, impulse, expectation? Considering it as related to desire, is it only temporarily unfulfilled or is there some impossibility, opposition, conflict? Considering it as an intention, is there any plan of action which could reasonably be expected to lead to its fulfilment? As desire or motive, is it necessarily positive, or may it equally be negative, that some event should *not* occur? The suspicion is aroused that he was working without a concept of omnipotence and meant something like the following: a wish is something that envisages its fulfilment without consideration of the means required for its accomplishment. If this is the case then the differentiation between night-dream and day-dream is eliminated in respect of mental functioning as a whole. Indeed one's final impression of Freud's attitude towards dreams is that they are of little interest to the dreamer himself, except in so far as they throw light upon his unconscious mental life in the same way that they are of interest to the psycho-analyst. They are to be taken as of evidential interest but not as life-events. But can one escape the impression that, say, "the dream of Irma's injection" was an event in Freud's life and deeply disturbed him, not just for the light it shed on his character but because it *happened*?

C. *Manifest and Latent Dream-content* – the great undertaking of demonstrating that dreams were not nonsense seems to have led Freud into a type of logical error, namely of confusing obscurity of meaning with cryptic or hidden meaning. He states clearly (p.277): "The dream-thoughts and the dream-content are presented to us like two versions of the same subject-matter in two different languages. Or, more properly, the dream-content seems like a transcript of the dream-thoughts into another mode of expression, whose characters and syntactic laws it is our business to discover by comparing the original and the translation." Of course the great difficulty is to obtain "the original", by which he means the thoughts being represented in the manifest content. In so far as he follows this mode of procedure, he is able to make wonderful headway in elucidating the dream-work, except when he insists on his cryptographic intent. We can see clearly that the two intentions, to understand and to solve, (as a puzzle or even as a crime) conflict seriously with one another and lead to all sorts of tricks for undoing the supposed trickiness of the dreamer *vis-à-vis* the dream censor.

D. *The Dream-censor* — it is difficult to remember that the enormously subtle and complex modes of thought which went into the works from *Mourning and Melancholia* onwards were not as yet in the character of the forty-four year old Freud, struggling with his own neurosis, isolated by his interests, clinging to the man, Fliess, who is so often and singularly referred to in these volumes as "my friend" while everyone else is only "a friend" or "a colleague". The man of the *Traumdeutung* was a Victorian, a Jew struggling for a place in the sun, taking for granted the mores and values of his community. The idea of conflict could not as yet find a place in his theories because there is no neurophysiological basis for such an idea. Accordingly the idea of a dream-censor was a very radical one indeed and suggested a mental structure for which no possible anatomical basis could be imagined. One must not think that he meant anything like the mental structure that would later be called "superego". Consider what a difference in conceptual framework is indicated by the addition (in brackets) made eleven years later to the following sentence (p.234): "Thus the wish to sleep (which the conscious ego is concentrated upon, and which, together with the dream censorship and the 'secondary revision' which I shall mention later, constitute the conscious ego's share in dreaming) must in every case be reckoned as one of the motives for the formation of dreams, and any successful dream is a fulfilment of that wish". A "wish to sleep" and a "conscious ego which is concentrated upon a wish to sleep" belong to very different models of the mind. A wish is no longer, in 1911, a physiological tendency whose fulfilment is sought; it is now something that an ego is "concentrated upon". Furthermore it can be seen as operating in conjunction with a dream-censor, not merely using devices to evade it.

But that is 1911; in 1900 the dream-censor is a rather fanciful term for the excesses of stimulation that could disrupt the sleep, as in unsuccessful dreams. In other words the argument is fairly tautological. If the dreamer remains asleep, the dream has been successful, which means that the dream-censorship has been evaded. If the thief enters and the dog does not bark at No.45 as it did at No.35, the thief has been quieter...or perhaps there is no dog at No.45. But that is not possible in a neurophysiological model; every house must have a dog.

This, in essence, is the theory, qua theory, the conceptual framework around which the wealth of observations and imaginative conjectures of this epoch-making book are woven. But as with the *Three Essays on Sexuality,* the editors of the Standard Edition have introduced historical confusion by coalescing the various editions through interpolation, even though they have usually indicated the dates of the later additions in brackets, or sometimes in footnotes. These latter are always referred to at the end of of the added paragraph or section, so that it is not clear where they start on the page. This creates great conceptual confusion, because the Freud who made additions (and possibly deletions – this is not made clear) in 1908, 1911 or 1914 is a very different man in more respects than theories. It is an enigma of psycho-analytical history that the theory of dreams, which is in so fundamental a way non-psycho-analytic, should have been preserved through the years in word while dishonoured in deed in every session where a dream plays a part. For there are no "Freudians" in the 1900 sense at the present time, so great has been the development in conceptual framework, most of it inaugurated by Freud himself in the transformation into Structural Theory.

In thus setting aside the "theory of dreams" as essentially uninteresting to practising psycho-analysts, it might be worthwhile to cite a single example of the insights which utterly negate the theory. (p.333): "The content of all dreams that occur during the same night forms part of the same whole; the fact of their being divided into several sections, as well as the grouping and number of those sections – all of this has a meaning and may be regarded as a piece of information arising from the latent dream-thoughts." Such a conception of dream-continuity (see Chapter XI below) cannot be brought into line with the momentary function of preserving sleep attributed to dreaming in the "theory". It is important to remember that what Freud means by "dream thoughts" are those thoughts of the "day-residue" of waking life which, by virtue of their link with early developmental history have a special disturbing effect on the dreamer's unconscious state. In this way dream-thoughts are taken as prior in existence to the dream itself. This is in keeping with a static conception of the unconscious because memory, as a mental function, is taken to mean something

14

like "storage" in the modern sense of computer construction. Yet Freud himself had discovered, at the time of the collapse of the "seduction theory" of hysteria, that memory, unlike recall, is dynamic and reconstructive, subject to all manner of incompleteness, distortion, coalescence and addition.

Perhaps it would not labour the argument too much to cite one other factor in Freud's thinking that may help us to understand his attitude to dreams in 1900. (p.312): "...dreams have no means at their disposal for representing these logical relations ("if, because, just as etc. without which we cannot understand sentences") between the dream-thoughts. ...The plastic arts of painting and sculpture labour, indeed, under a similar limitation." He might just as well have added music if he thought that all music was "programmatic" as he seems to have thought of the plastic arts as telling a story. We can see that thought and language were quite indistinguishable to him and that verbal thought stood as the primary symbolic form for representing meaning. In fact in the text he promptly goes on to illustrate the many ways in which dreams do in fact represent logical relationships between the individual thoughts.

All in all the essential poverty of the theoretical framework of the book is due mainly to preconception and seems to contrast with the astonishing richness of the observations and ideas thrown up around them. One is reminded of the story of the slothful sons whose father, in leaving them his lands, told them that his gold was buried somewhere one foot underground. Freud, in his search for "security, wealth and lasting fame", seems to have behaved like these sons. The real harvest of the *Traumdeutung* is to be found in Chapter VI on the "dream-work" to which we may now turn our attention with pleasure and relief.

E. *The Dream-work* – Chapter VI of the dream book is of endless fascination for its wealth of observation and acute thought, marred only by the editorial hodge-podge and perhaps the paternalistic handing out of honours to the faithful and the scourging of poor Stekel. But Freud-the-person obtrudes in a most disturbing way through the presentation of his own dreams and the associations connected with them. One is always inclined to point to this aspect of the *Traumdeutung* as an example of Freud's fearlessness in pursuit of the truth and perhaps to place him analogically with those great medical pioneers who first experimented upon themselves at the risk of their very lives. Doubtless there is truth in this and it does no more dishonour to him to consider other aspects than it would to suggest that some depressive conflict operated in Koch or Pasteur. For one is also struck with Freud's naïvety in revealing so much of his private mental life. It is true that he never reveals any *event* that would place him in disrepute, but he does reveal weaknesses, anxieties, motives and emotions of which no person could be proud. To what purpose? He had ample supplies of dreams and analyses thereof to fill out his book. Surely there was no special validity to be claimed from investigation of his own dreams; in fact, on the contrary, they were open to the charge that all the forces of the censorship would be operative in the form of resistance in the waking Freud. Indeed the impression is very often quite distinct. (p.437): "It is to be observed that the dream was allowed to ridicule my father because in the dream-thoughts he was held up in unqualified admiration as a model to other people. It lies in the very nature of every censorship that, of forbidden things, it allows those which are *untrue* to be said rather than those which are true."

What then are we to make of these autobiographical sallies? They are not so surprising in a senior and distinguished person writing his memoirs, where such revelations of weakness only highlight the many virtues coyly hinted at. But in this isolated and lonely man of 1900, it seems incomprehensible. His character was already considerably under attack from establishment figures and even his mentor, Breuer, had turned away, as the dream just mentioned above clearly reminds us, for Breuer is the figure of ridicule screened by the unreservedly admired father. One answer to this enigma is hinted at above, namely that Freud had the idea that dreams could never speak the truth directly – only indirectly, like a newspaper under a tyrannical regime. But probably the more important answer is that he did not believe that dreams could say anything *new* at all.

It is for this reason that the discussion of the dream-work in Chapter VI seems so often paradoxical in its development. In almost every section the theoretical statement that introduces the subsection is then refuted by the examples that follow. In a sense it would almost qualify for the term "absurd" as Freud uses it to describe the apparent paradoxes and nonsensical aspects of the manifest content of certain dreams, such as the one about "his father's drunkenness in 1851" from which the quotation above has been taken. Thus from the standpoint of the "theory of dreams" the chapter on dream-work is an investigation of a meaningless process, one in which meaning is, if anything, destroyed rather than created or augmented.

Perhaps this enigma, of Freud's insistence that all intellectual activities that appear in the manifest content of dreams are derived from the fragments of waking thoughts that lie behind, is most striking in the analysis of the dream of "the dissection of his own legs" (p.453). The use of autobiographical material in his work, that is, his self-analysis itself as well as the bits of it revealed in his writings, is here represented as his having to dissect his own legs under the order of his laboratory chief from neuro-physiology days, Brücke. Clearly in the analysis of the dream his bitterness about this degree of invasion of his own privacy and the exposure to ridicule to which it, along with the theories themselves, was exposing him, finds a virulent expression. But he also traces the infantile root to hatred of the parents for excluding the small child from their sexual intimacy. Does it all perhaps suggest the continued submission to a neurophysiology-father whose tyranny is still active in the forty-six year old Freud? The fact that this dream took place during a train journey links it with the travel phobia to which he makes reference in many places. At any rate we can conjecture that it cost him some considerable internal struggle to liberate himself from the neurophysiological preconceptions of the Fliess period and the "Project for a Scientific Psychology" in order eventually to emerge as a phenomenological psychologist who could acknowledge that the past was present in the *structure* of the personality and not merely buried as "recollections" in the repressed unconscious.

Section H of the chapter on the dream-work comes to the heart of the matter, "Affects in Dreams", and clarifies Freud's theoretical position on affects better than anywhere else in his writings. It is clear that he viewed affects as *manifestations* of meaning and not as *containers* of meaning. In this he was following the Darwinian line which traced emotions in man to the *expression* of emotions in more primitive animals, and thus seriously confused the *experience* of emotion with its *communication*. (p.460): "Our feelings tell us that an affect experienced in a dream is in no way inferior to one of an equal intensity experienced in waking life, and dreams insist with greater energy upon their right to be included among our *real* [my italics] mental experiences in respect of their affective than in respect of their ideational content. In our waking life however, we cannot include them in this way because we cannot make any *psychical assessment* [my italics] of an affect unless it is linked to a piece of ideational material. If the affect and the idea are incompatible in their character and intensity, our waking judgment is at a loss". Clearly "our feelings tell us" something very different from our "waking judgment" and the problem lies in the decision about priority in mental functioning between "feelings" and "waking judgment". Freud deprives feelings of the significance of judgment and therefore cannot allow affects, whether dreaming or waking, the status of "mental experiences" in themselves, but only as derivatives of "ideational material". It is natural for him therefore to deal with affects as something that can be separated from its appropriate ideational content, the latter being subjected to displacements and distortions, thus creating paradoxical conjunctions of the two. (p.463): *"Analysis shows us that the ideational material has undergone displacements and substitutions whereas the affects have remained unaltered"*. (Freud's italics)

Let us examine this idea in action in the brilliant analysis of the "open-air closet" dream. It runs thus: (p.468) *"A hill, on which there was something like an open-air closet: a very long seat with a large hole at the end of it. Its back edge was thickly covered with small heaps of faeces of all sizes and degrees of freshness. There were bushes behind the seat. I micturated on the seat; a long stream of urine washed everything clean; the lumps of faeces came easily away and fell into the opening. It was as though at the end there was still some left"*. His associations and interpretations trace the megalomania about his discoveries of the infantile aetiology of the neuroses, thus comparing himself with Hercules in the Augean stables, with Gulliver in Lilliput, etc. But also he sees the Gargantuan theme of revenge upon the audience to his lecture of the previous day as representing the forces determining his "grubbing about in human dirt", epitomized by one flatterer who indeed had compared him with Hercules – to Freud's great revulsion. (p.470): "The content of the dream had to find a form which would enable it to express both the delusions of inferiority and the megalomania in the same material. The compromise between them produced an ambiguous dream-content; but it also resulted in an indifferent feeling-tone owing to the mutual inhibition of these contrary impulses."

The presentation of this little gem is preceded by the qualification, "a short dream, which will fill every reader with disgust". In saying this Freud immediately confuses the reader and the dreamer, but also the waking Freud with the sleeping man having a "real mental experience". What he calls an "indifferent feeling-tone" is surely the consequence of his comparing the complacency of the dream-micturator with the emotional response to the image in the waking man. What man, after all, has not noticed the complacency of a little boy in himself as he lavaged with some success a soiled lavatory pan? The adult man of the previous day had noticed in himself the interplay of megalomania about his achievements and revulsion at the work from which it was derived. But what he had not noted, and what the dream revealed, was the infantile complacency of successfully sweeping away all the rubbish that had been written on the subject by the "great" figures of his science. Well, almost swept away, for "there was still some left". Complacency, after all, is the prime affect inhabiting the correspondence of mutual commiseration between himself and Fliess of this period.

So we might suggest that Freud has seized upon the wrong problem in presenting this dream. It is not, (p.468) "Why did I feel no disgust during this dream?" but "How has the dream-work found such a telling representation for the affect of complacency?" In order to ask that question the waking examiner of the dream would need to start with two ideas which were indeed foreign to Freud. One would be the acknowledgement that dreaming is indeed a mode of "real experience" of life, and the other would have to be the acceptance of affects as genetically prior to ideational content. Neither of these was available to him because of his preconception about the waking origin of all the dream-thoughts. (p.467): "Whenever there is an affect in the dream it is also to be found in the dream-thoughts. But the reverse is not true. A dream is in general poorer in affects than the psychical material from the *manipulation of which it has proceeded.*" [my italics] This is his primary thesis, that dreams merely manipulate prior psychical material and the conclusion concerning affects follows with logical force. (p.468): "The inhibition of affects, accordingly, must be considered as the second consequence of the censorship of dreams, just as dream distortion is its first consequence". Here, it might be suggested, is the clearest revelation of the tautoglogical nature of Freud's "theory of dreams" and the most impressive explanation for the absence of a substantial theory of affects throughout his work.

Before we can close this discussion of the concept of the dream-work, with its four categories – displacement, condensation, symbol-formation and secondary-revision – it is necessary to backtrack to those aspects which we have skirted around in order to consider the central theme of the role of affects. Having done this, and having considered Freud's view of affects and his virtual incapacity to form a theory of emotions, we can look backwards and forwards, bringing together the ideas of displacement, condensation and secondary revision in a more coherent manner. The most disappointing aspect of Freud's thought lies in this sphere. (p.352): "Things that are symbolically connected today were probably united in prehistoric times by conceptual and linguistic identity." Clearly symbols are being given the same paleontological treatment that affects have been given, that is, they are to be treated as mere replacements of A by B on the basis of anachronistic non-thought, a kind of mental appendix, a codification trick for evading the censorship. (p.353): "As a rule the technique of interpreting according to the dreamer's associations leaves us in the lurch when we come to the symbolic element in the dream-content." The reason is that: "they frequently have more than one or even several meanings and as with Chinese script, the correct interpretation can only be arrived at on each occasion from the context."

A similar situation exists with the concept of condensation. Items in dream-thought are condensed, in Freud's view, merely by some semi-mechanical process of superimposition on the basis of similarity overall, or identity of items. There is no concern for meaning in this condensation but only for form and representability. (p.341): "Yet in spite of all this ambiguity, it is fair to say that the productions of the dream-work, which, it must be remembered, *are not made with the intention of being understood,*" (Freud's italics) "present no greater difficulties to their translators than do the ancient hieroglyphic scripts to those who seek to read them." This seems strange when one remembers how incomprehensible were the Egyptian hieroglyphics prior to the discovery of the Rosetta Stone. But the two images, of Chinese pictographic script and hieroglyphics, make it clear that Freud views the problem of understanding symbols as one of re-translation, since symbol-formation itself is seen as a process of translation, movement in form without alteration or increment in meaning. (p.345): "Indeed, when we look into the matter more closely, we must recognize the fact that the dream-work of this kind" (symbolization) "is doing nothing original in making *substitutions* [my italics] of this kind."

Having thus imposed a wallowing theory on a resistant material, so buoyant because the penetrating observations are so often coupled with brilliant clinical intuitions, Freud is forced to caulk the whole leaky structure with a shameful trick concept, that of "secondary revision". You might say he makes a virtue of his own pretension, the kind of hypocrisy wittily called "preaching what you practise". (p.490): "The thing that distinguishes it" (secondary revision) "and at the same time reveals this part of the dream-work, is its *purpose.*" (Freud's italics) "This function behaves in the manner which the poet maliciously ascribes to the philospher: it fills up the gaps in the dream-structure with shreds and patches." And here he finds himself suddenly in deep water indeed, having to consider the day-dream, unconscious day-dreams, unconscious thinking together with the evidence for the incredible speed at which the dream content unfolds. The neurophysiological model, having at its root the well-known slow rate of nerve-transmission, cannot cope with this speed. Of course in our own day espousal of the neurophysiological model, and the mind-brain equation, has recourse to the speed of the computer to by-pass this question, forgetting this knowledge that nerves do not transmit in the manner of electric wires with the speed of light. Freud's tricky solution envisages, in relation to Maury's famous "guillotine dream", (p.496), "a phantasy which had been stored up in his memory for many years and which was aroused – I would rather say 'alluded to' – at the moment at which he became aware of the stimulus which woke him" (the piece of wood which fell on his neck). "The key-phrase serves as a port of entry through which the whole network is simultaneously put in a state of excitation."

We cannot take leave of the Freud of 1900 without some examination of the revision of his ideas which followed later in his life, and in doing so to take note of the famous Chapter VII. Perhaps the transitional period of circa 1914 illustrates the dilemma in which he found himself with respect to his original theory. The irritability with which he resisted recognizing the need for revision highlights the central problem. The 1914 addendum to Chapter VI includes a discussion of Silberer's work on "the very act of transforming dream-thoughts into images" in which that author divided the phenomena he observed into two categories, "functional" and "material", the former expressing the state of mind of the dreamer, and the latter his dream-thoughts in the sense of day-residues.

Freud writes, after citing some examples, "The 'functional phenomenon',' the representation of a state instead of an object', was observed by Silberer principally in the two conditions of falling asleep and waking up. It is obvious that dream-interpretation is only concerned with the latter case". That is, it is obvious if one starts with the premise that the function of dreams is to prevent the sleeper from awakening. It is worthwhile quoting at length the irritable refutation of Silberer's claim to attention. (p.504): "Silberer has given examples which show convincingly that in many dreams the last pieces of the manifest content, which are immediately followed by waking, present nothing more nor less than an intention to wake or the process of waking. The representation may be in terms of such images as crossing a threshold ('threshold symbolism'), leaving one room and entering another, departure, homecoming, parting with a companion, diving into the water, etc. I cannot, however, refrain from remarking that I have come across dream-elements which can be related to threshold symbolism, whether in my own dreams or those of subjects whom I have analysed, far less frequently than Silberer's communication would have led one to expect.

"It is by no means inconceivable or improbable that this threshold symbolism might throw light upon some elements in the middle of the texture of dreams...in places, for instance, where there is a question of oscillation in the depth of sleep and of an inclination to break off the dream. Convincing instances of this, however, have not been produced. What seems to occur more frequently are cases of overdetermination, in which part of a dream which has derived its material content from the nexus of dream-thoughts is employed to represent *in addition* some state of mental activity.

"This very interesting functional phenomenon of Silberer's has, through no fault if its discoverer's, led to many abuses; for it has been regarded as lending support to the old inclination to give abstract and symbolic interpretation to dreams. The preference for the 'functional category' is carried so far by some people that they speak of the functional phenomenon wherever intellectual activities or emotional processes occur in the dream thoughts, although such material has neither more nor less right" (sic!) "than any other kind to find its way into a dream as residues of the previous day".

"We are ready to recognize the fact that Silberer's phenomenon constitutes a second contribution on the part of waking thoughts to the construction of dreams; though it is less regularly present and less significant than the first one, which has already been introduced under the name of 'secondary revision'." Freud then goes on to try to subsume the whole phenomenon under the rubric of self-observation and the concepts he had recently put forward in the paper "On Narcissism", thus by-passing the central problem of the symbolic representation of states of mind in the sleeper as a dream-activity which could not possibly be attributed to the mere finding of pictorial representation for day-residues. There can be little doubt that Silberer's evidence that the sleeper had a state-of-mind and that it found symbolic representation in the dream-process threatened the whole structure of Freud's theory that the "dream-work is doing nothing original".

It seems fairly certain, judging from the fact that he continued to revise the *Traumdeutung* as late as 1925, that Freud never completely resigned the preconceptions upon which his theory of the dream-process was founded. Although it is hedged again and again in footnotes and later writings, as we shall soon discuss, so much of his model of the mind was founded upon the cross-reference between dreams and the psychoneuroses, that he could hardly have abandoned one without the other toppling over from lack of support. The basic thesis of the "two principles of mental functioning" (as he later called it) that is, the economic principles of pleasure and reality, plus the essential distinction between the primary process in the unconscious (the systematic unconscious as distinct from the dynamic or descriptive unconscious) and the secondary process in the conscious and preconscious, found a clear-cut expression in Chapter VII which he was never to abandon.

Having skilfully "been able to find a place in our structure for the most various and contradictory findings of earlier writers" (p.592), Freud goes on in the section on "Primary and Secondary Processes" to stake out his position that "everything that we have described as the 'dream work' seems to depart so widely from what we recognize as rational thought-processes" as the basis for characterizing the mentality of the unconscious. In doing so it is as if he has forgotten that the basis for this conviction is fundamentally two-fold. In the first instance it is based on the hypothesis of an (invisible) dream-censor, for whose existence he has in fact adduced no evidence, and in the second on the equally unsubstantiated hypothesis that dreams are the guardians of sleep, against which he himself acknowledges the mass of evidence. Add to these two hypotheses the strong evidence for day-residues and for infantile memories, and one has a perfect recipe for a tautological argument. It would go something like this: since we find that the manifest content of dreams has discernible links with some events of the previous day and with childhood, as demonstrated by the patient's associations, it follows that these residues and memories are creating a tension in the system which must be relieved by some means if sleep, which we assume is a state of mental quiescence and withdrawal from external stimuli, is to be preserved. But how is this to be done without action, unless some trick is used to deceive the system in tension into the belief that its direction of striving has been satisfied? As there is a censor who will not allow even such stimulated gratification, these in their turn must be disguised to appear absurd. But this would not satisfy the requirements of the organ of consciousness in its craving for logical narrative structure, so a secondary revision is further required to make the dream acceptable to all parties concerned.

We can say therefore that it is a theory built upon a neurophysiological, energetic model of the mind, that it treats its hypotheses as if they were observed facts and clings to its untenable position with all the tricks that it attributes to the dream-work itself. It is not a theory of dreams, it is a theory of personality functioning in a complex social situation and will later be restated as the Structural Theory in *The Ego and the Id*.

23

II

The Epistemological Problem
in the Theory of Dreams

While the psycho-analytical literature has almost without exception followed Freud's lead in the general theory of dreams both as
regards their function in the mind as well as the mode of their
genesis, the literature of philosophy has been occupied, in so far
as it has taken note of the phenomenon of dreams at all, with the
epistemological aspect. This seems to take the form of two
different sorts of questions: can we know that we are dreaming?
and do dreams, as our prime evidence of a world of intuitive
mental activity, generate knowledge?

In general the interest in linguistics among the philosophers has
centred on defining the limits of language on the assumption that
language is both man's unique differentiating capacity that sepa-
rates human from animal mentality, and the parallel dicta that
anything that can be thought can be said, and anything that can be
said can be said clearly (Wittgenstein of the *Tractatus*). This attitude separated the world of rational thought about observable
facts from the world of emotion and intuitive understanding by
arrogating meaning exlusively to the former realm. This was not
meant to imply that the latter realm was of no importance in
human relations but that it did not deal with knowledge and therefore was meaningless in the epistemological sense. It rightly, in a
sense, relegated dreams to the vicinity of myths, religions, art as
the realm of the ineffable, where this term, meaning inexpressible
in words, equated this deficiency of language with the borderline
between real and mystical experience. But it wrongly mistook the
solipsistic position that one cannot have knowledge of other minds
with the parallel assumption that a mind cannot have direct
knowledge of itself.

The unmistakable link between this philosophical position and
Freud's attitude towards dreams is apparent in their common view
of the emotions. The idea that words which are intended to
describe emotions are in fact no better than evocative noises and
therefore "symptoms" of feeling rather than names for feelings,
deprives them alike of the status of either signs or symbols. It

24

certainly is true that our language is very feeble in this area and the whole world of the arts has grown up to augment this deficiency. But it is a foolish oversimplification to think that lyric poetry is merely painting pictures with words or making music with meaningless words, and thereby to deny to the various art forms their stature as non-discursive symbolic forms. It also leaves the problem of the generating of meaning up in the air, to be settled by the gestalt psychologists as a brain function of pattern-perception. In so far as language development is regarded as naming the perceptible patterns, and thus of sensible forms in the outside world, only the lexical aspect of language is even touched upon. The syntactic aspect would remain a complete mystery and would lead one to expect that primitive peoples should have languages that were in proportion in grammatical simplicity to their stage of cultural development. This in fact does not at all appear to be the case. It would also suggest that sign langauge would have appeared in human evolution prior to verbal language, which also is not the case. Among the American Indian tribes, linguistic divergence was so considerable that a sign language for inter-tribal communication developed which was in all respects adequate for describing the external world as they knew it, a world of objects, actions and patterned relationships between objects. It utilized the technique of epitomizing, that is the representation of differentiating features, a linguistic basis that has no similarity to verbal language and its genesis, with the rare exception of onomatopoeia. Denotation may be used in the teaching of language but it is not an intrinsic element in its genesis.

Observation of language development in children is a very complicated business, for the child's urge to language formation and usage is given its formal elements both by identification processses and by denotative teaching by the parents. Nonetheless the child's relation to the world as a world of external objects is clearly secondary in interest to his preoccupation with emotional relations, particularly to parents as objects of emotive significance. Undoubtedly the child emits certain noises which are symptomatic of its state of mind and these may be intuited by the parent, but this process lies outside its urge-to-communicate. It is an unmistakable phenomenon that the small child begins to make the music of discursive speech long before it can pronounce individual words other than those few primal naming attempts such as mama and da-da. The process of lalling or playing with vocal processes bears a striking connection with other processes of play, and these we certainly know deal with its emotional relationships and its attempts to think about them. Similarly its earliest communications of the discursive pattern are clearly intended to communi-

25

cate complicated states of mind, so that the denotative function may be reserved for gestures long after a considerable language ability has been achieved. "Don't point, dear; tell mummy what you want." The music of command, inquiry, triumph, accusation and the rest is heard ringing through the house long before individual words make themselves clear. It is no wild speculation to infer from the genesis of speech in children something of the internal logic of development that must have held true for the species, that language was originally developed as a song-and-dance procedure for the communication of emotional states of mind which later came to embrace the description of the non-human environment in so far as this world of perceptible forms, in the gestalt sense, came to be enveloped by the emotive meaning of the human relationships. Perhaps we need to be reminded in this age of science and materialism that interest in the external world as phenomenon is an extremely recent historic event that dates from the decay of religious fervour and its anthropomorphic view of the universe. Perhaps even "anthropomorphic" is too sophisticated a description; better say ethnocentric view of the universe, the universe of group mentality.

Philosophers in more recent years have moved in a direction that alters the view of the senselessness of the emotive aspects of human mentality. The later Wittgenstein of *The Philosophic Investigations*, Cassirer of *Symbolic Forms*, Susanne Langer of *Philosophy in a New Key* among others have moved from the equation of word and symbol in a direction that views symbol-formation as the heart of the matter and its diverse forms as the prime object of study. This means that the problem of meaning has been widened from a view that placed it as a fact of external reality which had to be *apprehended,* to a more internal position as something to be *generated* and deployed, a neo-Platonic view. This move has accompanied the tendency away from the view that the mind is the brain, in favour of a vision that places human mentality at a different phenomenological level from animal neurophysiology, with symbol-formation and the generating of meaning, and thus the possibility of discovering significance, as the central object of epistemological study.

This newer trend in philosophy, along with such unifying attitudes towards human mentality as underlies modern anthropology or Noam Chomsky's search for a universal generative grammar, highlights the essential mysteriousness of mentality that sets it apart from information gathering and sorting which the computer sciences and cybernetics have developed to such a high degree with modern mathematical tools. But it has also weakened the distinction between consciousness and unconscious mental processes. The traditional view in philosophy which was strengthened by Freud's view of primary and secondary process assumed an equation between consciousness and rationality. It is not coincidental that Wittgenstein found so much in Freud that accorded with his basic attitudes when one considers Freud's readiness to think of dreaming as devoid of thought, judgment and intrinsic language functions. The key to this area of agreement lies not only in the attitude towards dreams but in the view that emotions are merely symptomatic of states of mind rather than the meaningful core of the experience which requires transformation into symbolic form in order for it to be thought about and communicated to fellow creatures. Perhaps the only psycho-analyst who has written extensively about dreams to take a quietly divergent view from Freud's has been Ella Sharpe. It must certainly have been done so quietly in her book on *Dream Analysis* that hardly any notice has been taken of it. Her central creative contribution to the theory of dreams was to point out the mountains of evidence that dreams utilize what she chose to call the "poetic diction" of lyric poetry. By this she meant that dreams employ the many devices of simile, metaphor, alliteration, onomatopoeia etc. by which the language of poetry achieves its evocative capacity. She could have added to her list the qualities of ambiguity that William Empson outlined, the musical attributes which Susanne Langer described, the reversal of perspective of Wilfred Bion and many other devices of which we as yet know little in respect of dreams but which have been identified as aesthetic devices in the various art forms.

This takes us back to the epistemological problems which not only include the question, "Can I know that I am dreaming?" but also, "Can I know what someone else has dreamed?" Freud perhaps paid too little attention to the distinction between dreaming and remembering a dream, and almost no attention to the problem of listening to someone else's account of his dream. In the dream book the examples of patients' dreams are given exactly the same status for purposes of exposition as examples of the author's own. The short shrift he afforded Silberer's "transition phenomena" also shows that he was unable to concern himself with the question of sleep as a phenomenon of variable depth or completeness. When is someone "completely" asleep, or "deeply" so, as compared to "dozing" or "half-asleep"? Had he taken greater heed of his own definition of consciousness as an "organ for the perception of psychic qualities", he would have had very little difficulty in framing a directional definition in regard to this organ's orientation towards external and internal phenomena, even if he had not taken such a concrete view of psychic reality as Melanie Klein embraced. Certain philosophers (Norman Malcolm, for instance) seem to be disturbed by the possibility of a sleeping person being able to answer the question put to him, "Are you awake?" with a negative answer. Where waking and consciousness are equated, of course, this would be so paradoxical as to seem merely a joke. But to draw the conclusion that a person cannot know he is asleep and therefore that nothing rational can go on in that state is, epistemologically speaking, a tautological matter of definition rather than of observation. Of course we "know" that we are asleep and many dreamers report that incipient anxiety in a dream is sometimes allayed by assuring themselves that they are asleep and dreaming. Of course the meaning of being attacked in a dream is different from the meaning of being attacked in the outside world, so that the reassurance that it is "only" a dream marks this distinction but does not imply that the attack is meaningless, without significance or without consequences for the dreamer. We may be half-asleep and in doubt about this directional aspect of our experience, or we may be so taken aback by an external world experience that we momentarily question its validity, especially if its configuration is one that touches closely some familiar pattern of our dream-life. But this is not the same as the problem that arises from the extreme and sometimes haunting impact that certain dreams may have. The developmental consequences of the wolf-dream for Freud's Russian nobleman was not produced by any uncertainty as to the external reality of the image of those wolves in the tree.

But even if we take Freud's view as denying that we have "experiences" in our sleep and only admitting that we work over in sleep the experiences of waking life, we would have to say that it is a position which denies psychic reality to our dream-life and object-significance to the personae of our dream world. It might correspond, for instance, to Wordsworth's "emotion recollected in tranquillity"* and in this way assign to dreams a contemplative function. Freud's definition of thought as experimental action would fit well with this and give to the dream-life what "withdraw and regroup" gives to military life. But if we are to allow that "meaning" goes beyond the perception of gestalten and that mental life goes beyond anything that one could imagine as a property of computers, we would need to embrace the concept "mystical" at a level which in no sense views it as a peculiar property of the few, a minute fraction of whom have made some impact on human history, the rest having been *too* mad. We would need to take this concept seriously as implying the possibility that mentation is non-sensuous in its inception, that it is concerned with objects for whom forms need to be invented or borrowed from external reality, that

*Lyrical Ballards, preface.

has emotion as its central phenomenon and whose laws are not those of logic or mathematics but of "progression" in formal qualities (Langer), or "transformation" (Bion).

In writing this I become increasingly aware of the magnitude of the task undertaken in this book and, with that, the impossibility of doing more than laying a groundwork of a new theory of dreams. Clearly I am attempting to formulate an aesthetic theory of dreams against the philosophical background outlined above and on the foundations of that line of psycho-analytical thought, presented in *The Kleinian Development*, that envisages a progression in model-of-the-mind from Freud through Klein to Bion. This word 'aesthetic' may come as a surprise and be mistaken as an aspiration towards framing a theory which has beauty in its integration. That is not my aim; I mean to outline a theory about dreams which takes the view that they are essentially the function of the mind which deals with our aesthetic experience of the world where "beauty is truth, truth beauty". Melanie Klein's description of development in terms of an original paranoid-schizoid position giving way gradually to a depressive orientation is not one that has been borne out by infant observation, psycho-analytic therapy or the studies with autistic children. Rather these studies suggest strongly that emotional experience is essentially aesthetic and that the processes of the paranoid-schizoid position are instituted, from splitting-and-idealization onwards, by the urge to defend against the pains of the aesthetic experience of the beauty of the world, a world at first bounded by the mother's mind and body.

If we return for a moment to the question of language and other symbolic forms by which human beings attempt to communicate their experiences of the world to one another, we will find ourselves taking the view that all of these modes of communication are to be understood as ways of talking "about" the central emotional experience. We will be assuming that attention is deployed either towards or away from these experiences and that attention is the tiller by which we steer the organ of consciousness about in the teeming world of psychic qualities. We will be taking as our primary object of study what Wittgenstein called "seeing as" in a sense that goes far beyond the gestalt patterning and focuses our own attention on an area whose qualities are not merely ineffable processes of symbol-formation in Susanne Langer's sense of "presentational forms" as against discursive ones, or of Ella Sharpe's "poetic diction" as against Freud's view of "representability", "condensation" and "displacement".

Perhaps the best way of making this deceptively simple idea of "seeing as" more vivid would be to present some clinical material. In July of 1980 Martha Harris and I had the good fortune to hear some extraordinary observations made in the course of a therapeutic approach to an eighteen month old child. This lovely looking child was already causing concern, with the possibility of autistic development being mooted, because of his lack of desire to communicate, stereotyped hand movements, insomnia, asthmatic and colicky bouts, and a persistent inability to rise to the standing position without assistance. Once on his feet Giovanni tended to be in constant motion, walking back and forth in a straight line, only stopping occasionally to examine some non-existent spot on the wall. He never smiled, the parents reported, but neither did the mother, who clearly had been in a deeply depressed state since the post-operative death of her first-born little girl who had had congenital heart disease. Giovanni was conceived two months after this bereavement. The pregnancy and delivery were normal and he was fed at the breast for three months, feeding well but making no emotional contact with the mother. During the first year he had great difficulty sleeping and from three months on suffered from what seemed to be inconsolable distress, perhaps abdominal colicky pain, perhaps anguish of some sort.

I describe the first four sessions which the therapist had with this little boy, utilizing a technique based on psycho-dynamics amplified by considerations of gestalt perceptions of form. I will quote mostly from the English translation of her presentation.

First Session

The child goes backwards and forwards in the room, either from one side to the other or from one end to the other. He starts off quickly, as if about to walk a long distance, but suddenly he stops, turns about and goes back to where he started. He does not look around him, but every now and then he stops as if called, bends his head to one side as if searching for the voice, half-closes his eyes, and then continues walking. Suddenly he stops, makes a series of meaningless movements with his hands, and goes to the wall to stare at some non-existent spot.

I try to go near him, but he perceives me as an obstacle that has to be avoided. I call to him, as do his mother and father, but he pays no attention. I try touching him, stroking him. When I do this I can hear his breathing accelerate and he then makes puffing noises with his mouth and modulates this to a noisy dribbling. He has his dummy in his mouth but does not suck it.

Second Session

The parents, accompanied by the ten year-old brother, carry
Giovanni in and put him in my arms, mentioning that he had been
car-sick. The rest of the family leave without the child seeming to
notice. He has his dummy in his mouth. As I sit beside the sand-pit
with him in my arms and touch the sand, he vomits his milk and
begins to cry. I clean him, hold him tight and he calms down, beginning to suck his dummy, taking it from his mouth and then
replacing it. The family returns and seem vexed when told of the
vomiting. Mother picks Giovanni up saying, "He wants his
mummy". When finally put down, he commences his back and
forth perambulation, but when I make various noises like knocking, he stops each time. When I open the door into the long corridor, he immediately goes out, although it is quite dark. He continues his march, each time going a bit farther until he has walked
the length of the corridor.

When I call him he stops immediately, tries to lift his head to
look at me, but seems unable to manage this. So I kneel down. He
looks at me, comes near and, for the first time, smiles. The parents
are quite startled and say, "It is the first time he has ever smiled at
a stranger". I return from the corridor and sit on the carpet in the
room. Giovanni enters, seems to measure the space at a glance and
comes close. I stroke him and softly call his name, but each time he
is touched the acceleration of his breathing is noticeable. I gently
lay him down on the carpet and bend over him. He looks up and
down the length of my body. As I take the dummy from his mouth
and whisper his name and those of his family, he looks intensely
at me and moves his mouth as if in imitation. He seems very serene,
but when I move he tries to get up, rolling over, getting onto his
knees, but clearly cannot stand up. So I offer him my finger, which
he touches but then rejects, puffing and dribbling. I keep my
finger available and Giovanni touches it several times but cannot
seem to grasp it to help himself to stand. So I close his hand on my
finger and help him to get up. This seems to evoke the first sounds
he has made, a kind of ma-ma-ma lalling.

Third Session

Having been put down outside the entrance, Giovanni enters by
himself. When I approach and offer my finger for him to lead me,
he looks at it, touches it, tries to grasp it but immediately loses it.
So I place my finger in his palm and close his hand on it, feeling
his grasp tighten. He seems very calm as we proceed, his dummy
hanging by its gold chain rather than in his mouth. When I stop,

Giovanni stops and puffs, seeming to be a bit disappointed, but then precedes me into the room, where we both immediately sit down on the carpet. After a while I roll a large ball gently towards him, but he does not look at it and pushes it away when it touches him. However, when I lay him down on the carpet and place the ball between his hands, he grasps it, presses it hard to his chest and smiles brightly.

When I have removed the ball and Giovanni holds his hands out to me, I offer my face, but he begins to puff noisily and then starts to get up while I am speaking softly to him. He looks about for some aid to stand but soon takes my finger, rises and goes out into the corridor, beginning his back and forth promenade, now almost at a run. I fetch a large wooden ring and place it on the floor and when Giovanni comes level with it he stops suddenly, becoming rigid as he regards it, moving his head round and round and even begins to sway his body in the same way. I lift the ring from the floor with one hand while with the other I lift him and place him inside it. He accelerates his breathing, begins to puff, and when I place the ring on the floor, he steps out of it unaided.

Fourth Session

I have taken Giovanni in my arms towards the sink where he immediately began to play with the water, the dripping having apparently attracted his attention. When he first touches the water he immediately pulls back, puffing, but returns again and again, now with accelerated breathing but without puffing. This progresses over a fifteen minute period until, instead of rapid breathing or puffing, he stops breathing and becomes rigid. I let a small plastic fish drop into the water, but Giovanni immediately turns away and curls up in my arms, where in fact he seems to fall asleep. When his mother suggests that he wants his dummy, Giovanni wakes and wants to get down, beginning his running, hand-shaking and staring at the wall. But when I kneel down, call to him and open my arms invitingly, the mother does the same, receiving and cuddling the child.

When the child is put down and starts to run, I take the wooden ring and roll it slowly in the opposite direction to his running. He changes direction, comes up behind me and runs along moving his head round and round. When I offer my finger, he takes it firmly and walks beside me lalling again, but this time more like "pa-pa-pa", and "bu-bu". When I walk towards the room with the red carpet, he runs ahead of me and seems to test the carpet with his foot, but he immediately pulls it back. This is repeated several times, Giovanni on the perimeter and myself seated on the carpet.

He begins to pace the perimeter, panting, trembling, puffing, and I repeat his types of breathing. This seems to arrest his attention and he regards me, head to one side, then tries again to mount the carpet. When I hold out my finger he grasps it, puffs hard, cries out in distress... and then comes onto the carpet with me, into my arms where he curls up, quiet.

This breath-taking drama seems to reveal, sometimes as if in slow motion, other times as if highly accelerated, the transitions back and forth from one-, two- and three-dimensionality which must be a constant feature in the life of the normal new-born. Giovanni does indeed seem to present autistic-like states, with the one-dimensional running, the staring at nothing and the meaningless hand stereotypy. But it is noticeable that objects with formal qualities that may be taken to have at least a two-dimensional significance not only attract his attention, such as the ball, the ring, perhaps the finger, but not the face, evoke an immediate identificatory reaction. This primitive narcissistic mode which Esther Bick has described as "adhesive" can be seen in Giovanni's head and body movements when presented with the large wooden ring. But when he was placed inside it, immediate anxiety, which we tentatively label "claustrophobic", ensued. This anxiety seems to have been repeated when the little fish was dropped into the water, for it may very well not merely have represented an invader of his private space, but may also have drawn him into identification, as did the ring. This, in fact, was the therapist's impression. "Every time the water touches him it is as though he is completely immersed" and it is at those moments that he stops breathing and becomes rigid. We may conjecture that the fish entering the water could not be clearly distinguished from falling into it himself.

It would not seem to be too wild a stretch of the imagination to link the happy experience with the ball (which could not be transferred to the face), the experiment with the water (which was spoiled by the entry of the plastic fish), and the ordeal of the red carpet (which had been a perfectly happy place to play prior to the experience of being placed inside the wooden ring). Note that this experience with the ring was not geographically connected with the carpet, for it took place in the corridor. The first two episodes of anxiety and rejection (of the face that could not replace the ball, and of the water into which the plastic fish had entered) could easily have taken place with a baby monkey or even a puppy. In Kohler's experiments with apes he observed that if the young ape had the stick and the suspended banana in view simultaneously, he could make the connection and use the stick to reach the banana. But if the banana was in front of him and the stick behind, he could not make this tool-concept. Here we see a superior intelligence at work that can make a connection between a wooden ring that the child was placed inside several days before in a different location, and a red carpet on which he had happily disported himself a week previously. But the carpet has now changed; it has been overwhelmed by a new concept. It is being "seen as" a space with a perimeter, a two-dimensional area with a three-dimensional significance, scintillating with claustrophobic anxiety, and with great attractiveness. Here indeed is an example of new wine in old bottles, of an object taking on new meaning which leads to new significance. The red carpet had, through the mysterious processes of human mentality, been transformed from an external object with perceptible qualities into a symbol containing emotional meaning.

The theory of dimensionality which was outlined in *Explorations in Autism* runs parallel with Bion's great exposition of a theory of thinking and in a way supplements its developmental implications. In that book my colleagues and I traced the progression in dimensionality in the four children described. Here in four sessions Giovanni and the therapist have exposed the same process in an exquisitively condensed form. It allows us to attempt to discern the emotional experience which was worked upon by Bion's alpha-function to elevate the red carpet from external object to symbol of internal processes. We can safely assume that the central emotional experience, the one which so startled Giovanni's parents, was the one which manifest itself as a smile when the therapist kneeled down to the child's level so that he need not perform the seemingly impossible task of looking up at her as an object of attraction and interest. Certainly she had already engaged him with her finger assisting him to rise. (It is of interest that the mother reported that she always makes a chair available to him rather than her body for this feat.) It is surely significant that the dummy which had filled his mouth unsucked, underwent a series of alterations, being sucked, later dropped from his mouth and returned, and finally, in the third session, left hanging by its gold chain. This is the prelude to the experience of the ball which brought the bright smile. But while the therapist's face brought down to his level had evoked a smile, its presentation to his hands as an object equivalent to the ball induced anxiety. Could it be that her mouth, so interesting in its talking that it could evoke his lalling mimicry, was in another way too threatening? Might it swallow him as the water swallowed the little plastic fish, or as the red carpet might also do, so that its solid surface had to be tested repeatedly with his foot? Perhaps the unsucked dummy had a protective function, the guardian of his mouth. Or was it the protector of his object against his insatiable hunger that might devour the mother? Her insistence that he wanted his dummy and Giovanni's vomiting when the mother went away both suggest just such a collusion between them.

Clearly we are evolving a thesis that the emotional experience which evoked the two smiles, the common denominator, is essentially one of being offered an object (finger, face, attention, interest) rather than a substitute (a dummy, a chair, a depressed mother grieving for her dead daughter). But if the child cannot clearly distinguish between his own mouth as a focus of hungry desire, and a destructive maw, how is he to be sure of the therapist's mouth which makes such interested and interesting music? This, I would suggest, is the emotional experience, the conflict of desire and anxiety, which has found a symbolic representation in the red carpet. Through alchemy of the mind diverse items have been brought together in this representation: (a) the attractive form of the ball; (b) the form of the washbasin with its untrustworthy surface of water; (c) the red perimeter of the therapist's mouth; (d) the wooden ring into which he had been lifted but from which he escaped. Are we not immediately reminded of fairy tale images: the witch's house in Hansel and Gretel; the wolf-grandmother in Little Red Riding Hood? Ultimately, perhaps, the apple on the Tree of Knowledge of Good and Evil?

III

The Klein-Bion Expansion of Freud's Metapsychology

Sigmund Freud's genius was a child of its time and he was naturally preoccupied with the current scientific developments and psychotherapeutic methods. He wanted to create an explanatory science which could prove things. He naturally looked upon the mind and brain as phenomenologically identical and was preoccupied with a neuro-physiological model, with "hydrostatics", with the Darwinian framework of evolution applied to the mind. This model drew on comparative anatomy, embryology and, unfortunately, archaeology, backed by the First and Second Laws of Thermodynamics, to frame a metaphor which was mistaken for a theory. While these gave him tremendously useful tools they also imposed their limitations when treated as theoretical hypotheses requiring experimental proof.

This model of the mind, which is made explicit (as preconceptions) in the "Project for a Scientific Psychology", did indeed stay with him all his life. It was a model that was bound, by its own structure, to impose on him a view of mental life in which he could not possibly have believed but that he nonetheless used as a basis for scientific work. It viewed the life of the mind as bound to the body and its needs, and thus engaged upon finding means to gratify these needs without running into an absolute confrontation with the environment, human and non-human. Freud eventually also came upon evidence of another agency that the personality has to satisfy, that is the agency of the conscience, of the Superego. His picture of the personality was a slightly sad one as spelt out in *The Ego and the Id.* He pictured the Ego as serving three masters – the Id (the instincts), the outside world, and the Superego. Using all the tricks and devices of its intelligence to outwit these three masters, the Ego sought to find some kind of balance, a peaceful co-existence. When Freud later came to formulate the theory of the Life and Death Instincts, it appeared that the very purpose of life was to die peacefully. It does not matter that he could not possibly have believed this, but as a scientist he worked at his assumptions and hypotheses, pursued them relentlessly, and produced an imposing and substantial foundation for the science.

His greatest clinical discovery was, of course, the phenomenon of the transference but because of his neuro-physiological "hydrostatic" model of the mind, he was bound to view transference as a repetition of the past and therefore bound to think of neurotics as people "suffering from reminiscences". He could not think of them as people living *in* the past because such a concept could not find any representation in his model. He could think of them as being tormented by unassimilated painful experiences, analogous to foreign bodies, causing constant irritation in their minds – a kind of surgical model. We may remember that one of the few people to appreciate his earliest book, *Studies in Hysteria,* referred to his method as a "surgery of the soul". Later, under the Structural Theory, the Superego could be viewed as a vestigial organ of the mind, in need of dissolution – an embryological model.

This concept of the transference as an emanation of the past was also accompanied, necessarily, by a view of dreams which could not see dreams as *dream life*, but merely as brain activities serving a fairly trivial function, supporters of the neurophysiological process of sleep. Although dreams could be appreciated as a splendid source of information for the understanding of personality, they could not have assigned to them a life function. Freud could not, therefore, even though he evolved a concept of Superego and spoke of internalization, come to a concept of an *internal world*. He could use that term only in an allegorical way. We can see in his work that he had opportunities for its more concrete use in the Schreber Case where the world destruction fantasy obtruded, for Freud realized that the world that Schreber destroyed was not the outside world but something in his mind. Freud could not, however, because of his basic model, find a place to locate this internal world. This in turn prevented him from coming very close to the problem of mental *health* because his model of the mind could only clearly examine mental *illness*. At the very end of his life, in his great imaginative and speculative paper, "Splitting of the Ego in the Service of Defence", he did make an attempt to break with the concept of "Unity of the Mind" imposed by the one-to-one neuroanatomical equation of mind and brain. This approach to transforming himself from a neuro-physiological psychologist into a phenomenological one can also be glimpsed in papers on fetishism and masochism – especially in "A Child is Being Beaten", where there is more freedom of imagination and concern with the meaning of things, and less emphasis on the distribution of energy and the attainment of what Cannon later called "homeostasis".

Freud also had difficulty, because of his basic model, in thinking of emotionality as the heart of the matter of mental life. He could

37

think of emotionality only in a Darwinian way as a relic of primitive forms of communication. He therefore, as it were, confused the *experience* of emotion with the *communication* of emotion; thus treating it as an *indicator* of mental functioning rather than as a function itself, much like a noise-in-the-machine.

These limitations of Freud's neurophysiological model of the mind highlight the significance of Melanie Klein's work. Its surprisingly revolutionary consequences were implied early in her career as an outgrowth of her listening naïvely to young children talking about the inside of their own and of their mothers' bodies. Freud could not adopt such naïvety when hearing of Little Hans talking about the same thing, telling his father about how, before he was born, he and his sister Hanna had ridden in the stork-box together, and had a relationship which was broken up by his birth. Freud could not listen in this way because he did not have a model that could take cognizance of it; but Melanie Klein did listen, and in so doing made a discovery which contributed a revolutionary addition to the model-of-the-mind, namely that we do not live in one world, but in two – that we live also in an internal world which is as real a place of life as the outside world.

This gave an entirely new significance to the concept of phantasy, namely that unconscious phantasies were transactions actually taking place in the internal world. This, of course, gave a new meaning to dreams. Dreaming could not be viewed merely as a process for allaying tensions in order to maintain sleep; dreams had to be seen as pictures of *dream life* that was going on all the time, awake or asleep. We may call these transactions "dreams" when we are asleep, and "unconscious phantasies" when we are awake. The implication was that this internal world must be assigned the full significance of a *place*, a life-space, perhaps *the* place where meaning was generated. Freud's formulation of the Superego could be expanded and transformed into the concept of internal objects. Psychic reality could be treated in a concrete way as a place where relationships were taking place and where the meaning of life was generated for deployment to the outside world.

This transformation to a Platonic view is absolutely implicit in Melanie Klein's earliest work and it transformed her psychoanalysis at that point from a Baconian science, aiming at explanations and hoping to arrive at absolute truths or laws, into a descriptive science, observing and describing phenomena that were infinite in their possibilities because they were phenomena of imagination and not the finite events of the distribution of the 'mental energy' of the brain. This *geographic* aspect of a model-of-the-mind, views mental phenomena as arising at a different phenomenological level from those of the brain, though obviously completely dependent in a "carrying" way on brain-body functioning.

Melanie Klein's evocation of the mental geography surprisingly revealed what might be called a theological aspect of the personality. Every person has to have a "religion" in which his internal objects perform the function of gods – but it is not a religion that derives its power from belief in these gods but from the functions these gods actually perform in the mind. Therefore if a person does not put his trust in them to perform these functions he must undertake them himself. Here the relative inadequacy of the self leaves him in the lurch (the organizational concept of narcissism). In other words Melanie Klein, without completely recognizing it, transformed "Narcissism" from a theory about the nature of the Libido and its attachment to the body into a concept that is a much more social and organizational one. It finds that the phenomenology of narcissism arises from the relationships of the child parts of the personality *to one another* in psychic reality in so far as they are in competition with, or in defiance of the internal objects, those parental figures who perform godlike functions.

This *geographical* dimension of an expanded metapsychology implied that the concept of transference was altered. Instead of transference phenomena being seen as relics of the past they could now be viewed as externalizations of the immediate present of the internal situation, to be studied as psychic reality. Neurotics would not be seen as "suffering from reminiscences" but could be thought of as *living in the past*, represented in the immediate present qualities of the internal world. The narcissistic organization stands in appostion to the object relations in a very similar way to that in which atheism stands in relation to theism. In other words if a person does not put his trust in his internal gods, he must live in a state described so vividly by Kierkegaard as "despair".

In Melanie Klein's early work this appostion appears as those emotional situations which she called the paranoid-schizoid position in which a person is bound to abandon himself to a value system of self interest, while in the depressive position concern for the good object is predominant over self-interest. This then was yet another revolutionary aspect of her work for it introduced values into the psycho-analytic view of the mind. Freud's view of science had required their exclusion to forestall any psychoanalytic "weltanschauung" which, he feared, would turn the science into a cult.

These were, in a sense, the main changes in the model of the mind that Melanie Klein's discoveries contained implicitly, though they were never spelled out as alterations or even as amendments to Freud's model. She describes a mind that deals with meaning, that deals with values, that oscillates in its relationships between narcissism and object relationships, that lives in at least two worlds, the outside world and the internal world. It is in the internal world of relationships that meaning is generated and deployed to relationships in the outside world.

This then is where her work stood until, in 1946, in "Notes on some Schizoid Mechanisms" she described the two mechanisms of *splitting* and *projective identification*. The study of the phenomena related to these two mechanisms remained the constant preoccupations of her students for the next thirty years. These two mechanisms describe the ways in which the mind destroys its own primal unity. Melanie Klein's expansion of Freud's description of splitting of the ego implied that a person lives multiple lives, in greater or less harmony and integration with one another. The bringing together of these splits is a very arduous and painful process involving the transformation of values from the paranoid-schizoid position to a depressive orientation. The concept of projective identification further complicated the model by multiplying the number of "worlds" that various parts of the mind may inhabit by adding the regions of "inside" objects to the duality of internal and external worlds. This had important implications for understanding difficulties of communication. Inhabitants of different worlds misunderstand one another because the language that they use has a different frame of reference. She demonstrated that to live in the inside of an object is to live in another world; it is not only a world that is different from either psychic reality or external reality, but it is a world of very severe disturbance, though not identical to the delusional system of the schizophrenic.

This idea of a complex geography of mental space throws a very bright light on certain aspects of dreams and pathological mental states. Recent experiences in analytic work for instance, suggest that the inside of the mother's body is generally divided into at least three areas that have very different meanings and very different organizations. The state of mind engendered in a part of the personality inhabiting each of these different compartments constitutes living in very different worlds.

The acute psychotic illness of a young man, who moved from one to another of these three worlds, illustrates beautifully the three different arenas of life that exist inside the internal mother's body.

A twenty year old youth, in a South American city, took off his clothes in the middle of the square and disappeared into the sewers; when police brought him out and took him to a mental hospital he told them that he had done this in order to escape from Hitler who was trying to enlist him for the SS. He spent about three months in this hospital during which time he became increasingly disturbed in a very particular way. He gradually began to complain that the place smelled foul; that the food was unclean, if not poisoned; that there were very sadistic things going on, particularly down in the basement whence he could hear screams. Gradually the atmosphere became so intolerable to him that he escaped. About a month or two later he asked to be admitted to a hospital in another town. There he stayed for several months and during his stay he gradually developed a very different kind of accommodation. He began to complain that the place was scintillating with sexuality. Everyone, staff and patients alike, was having sexual relations, the atmosphere was electric with sexual excitement which was driving him to continual masturbation, and that there were even sexual practices with children down in the basement, the sounds of which he found particularly unbearable. So he escaped from that hospital also. After a month or two he returned voluntarily to the first mental hospital and there, over a period of months, yet another entirely different kind of adjustment appeared. Gradually he began to complain that the atmosphere was delicious... everything smelled beautiful and, as a result, he could not stop breathing all the time. He kept breathing, breathing, and became terribly worried and depressed that he was breathing too much, that he was taking up too much of this delicious atmosphere, because he heard from the basement the cries of babies who were not getting enough oxygen as a result of his over-breathing.

This story illustrates the various qualities of the different worlds inside the internal mother's body. There is the rectum, a smelly and sadistic place; then the mother's vagina and womb, which is a very erotic place, and finally there is this idyllic place inside the chest, breast, or head. This illustrates the concreteness of these worlds in which a part of the personality can live. Experiences there cannot be communicated because the words have a different frame of reference – "air", for instance.

Melanie Klein's work, because of these transformed concepts, brought value into the centre of the problem. The elaboration of the experiences of different worlds and of a dream life as against waking life in the outside world; of unconscious phantasies as thinking processes where meaning is generated, particularly as one can study it in dream life; all brought emotionality also into a central position. Emotionality in this model-of-the-mind could no longer be viewed as an archaic manifestation of primitive communication processes; it had to be dealt with as the heart of the matter of meaning. But on the other hand the kind of meaning that was involved in Melanie Klein's model seemed to be only the meaning of relationships; that is, her concept of splitting processes, being so bound to what could be visually represented in dreams, envisaged the personality as dividing into parts, each having a complete set of mental functions. Therefore in her work she was not in a position to investigate the separate Ego functions, but only the relations of the separate parts of the self to one another and to internal and external objects.

Conditions in which particular functions are disordered attracted Wilfred Bion, beginning with his investigation of schizophrenic patients and their difficulties in thinking. By tracing Melanie Klein's concepts of splitting processes and projective identification not only to personality structures, but to separate Ego functions such as thinking, memory, attention, verbalization, action, judgment, he explored the possibility that the mind could attack itself in very minute ways. He adduced evidence of the splitting off of particular mental functions, as well as the projection of bits of the personality containing these isolated functions into other objects. Such objects of projective identification could then be experienced as able to perform these split-off functions, while what was left of the self could no longer perform them. And then, utilizing this concept of minute splitting and projective attacks on the self's capacities, he began to investigate and elaborate a concept of thinking. What he did first was to separate *thoughts*, and the elaboration of thoughts, from *thinking* as the transformation of these thoughts. He then introduced a modification to Melanie Klein's emphasis on the baby's relationship to the breast and the mother as the great modulator of mental pain which enables the baby to proceed with its development.

Under Melanie Klein's model, the development of the mind resembles the unfolding of a flower when it is adequately nourished and free from parasites or predators. Bion took quite a different view; namely that the development of the mind is a complicated process which has to be structured every step of the way and cannot therefore be compared with the biological forms of growth that are determined by genetic history and implemented by hormonal systems. He thought that mental development was in a sense autonomous; that the mind builds itself, bit by bit, by "digesting" experiences.

Bion took the view that the mother has to perform functions for the baby – mental functions – which the baby can then learn to perform for itself by internalizing her. He formulated it in terms of the baby's relationship to the breast: essentially the baby, being in a state of confusion and having emotional experiences about which it cannot think, projects distressed parts of itself into the breast. The mother and her mind (experienced by the baby as her breast), has to perform the function of thinking for the baby. She returns to the baby those disturbed parts of itself in a state that enables thinking, and particularly dreaming, to come into existence. This he called alpha-function. He left it as an empty concept because he did not know how to fill it and he was not at all certain that it could be filled in by any substantial description.

This conception of the development of the baby's capacity to think implied that it is not only dependent on the mother's reverie to put order into chaotic experience, but also on her availability as an object for internalization. This has given new significance to the human infant's protracted period of helplessness, so non-adaptive on superficial consideration. By linking dependence with the experience of the absent object as the "first thought", Bion suggested a new, highly adaptive meaning for the long period of infantile helplessness, implying it is necessary for the internalization of the mother as a *thinking* object, not merely as a *serving* one. This gave new meaning to Freud's speculation about Primary Narcissism and new importance to Melanie Klein's dating of the onset of the depressive position.

His next move was to elaborate this scheme into a sort of Periodic Table, called the Grid, to try to describe how thoughts grow in complexity, abstraction and sophistication in the mind so that they can be used for manipulation in thinking. The basic level of thoughts proper in this Periodic Table (called Row C) is the one with which Melanie Klein's work is concerned: that is, the level of dreams, dream thoughts and what Bion called myths.

In this Periodic Table of the growth of thoughts Bion also suggested that there may be a parallel growth in the mind of something that is in the service of mis-understanding, of anti-thought, which is opposed to the discovery of truth, and which is essentially a system for generating lies: a kind of Negative Grid.

By juxtaposing the elaboration of truth and lies and attributing these functions to the good and bad breast (or Satanic part of the self) Bion gave a new meaning to what Freud had called the life and death instincts, and to what Melanie Klein had described in *Envy and Gratitude* as the confrontation of the good internal objects with the envious and destructive parts of the personality. They struggle for the mind of the child, much as Milton pictures Heaven and Pandemonium to be in conflict for domination of the mind of mankind.

Thus in Bion's schema for describing thinking processes, parts of the personality that are bound in dependence, and potentially

43

in a love relationship to the good object, are constantly being pulled away by lies to abandon their relationship to the truth. This is, then, the "Primal" source of mental illness. If, as he says, truth is the nourishment of the mind and lies are its poison, then the mind, given the truth, is able to grow and develop itself while, conversely, if poisoned by lies, then it withers into mental illness – which can be seen as a kind of death of the mind.

This juxtaposition of truth and lies also raises the level of concern with meaning to an aesthetic level. It helps to differentiate between different levels of relationship. These may reasonably be called the level of intimate relationships, the level of contractual relationships and the level of casual relationships. Mental health, and the development of the mind, derives from intimate relationships in which the primordial events are *emotional experiences*. Bion's work places emotion at the very heart of meaning. What he says in effect (and this is almost diametrically opposed to Freud's attitude towards emotion) is that the emotional experience of the intimate relationship has to be thought about and understood if the mind is to grow and develop. In a sense the emotion *is* the meaning of the experience and everything that is evolved in the mind through alpha-function such as dreaming, verbalizing dreams, painting pictures, writing music, performing scientific functions – all of these are *representations* of the meaning. This is another way of saying that the meaning of our intimate relationships is our passions, and that understanding our passions has the function, primarily, of protecting these passions from being poisoned and eroded by the lies that are generated by the destructive parts of the personality. Mental health consists, essentially, in being able to preserve this area of passionate intimate relationships, the aesthetic level of experience, of which the emotion itself is the meaning.

To illustrate this and to show a minute fragment of complex dream thinking, how it takes forms and functions from the outside world, mixes them with words from the outside world and uses them to represent the *meaning* of emotional experiences, I shall describe three dreams from a patient whose dreams seem to be particularly thoughtful.

The patient, a woman in her early forties, reported that around age thirteen, from being a very mediocre student and a nobody, she had found herself propelled through her outgoing qualities into eventually becoming Head Girl. The transformation in her personality which had taken place between the ages of thirteen and sixteen was maintained through University and after. At the age of forty she suffered a sudden illness and underwent surgery. Although the surgery was said to have been very successful and

44

the prognosis was good, she was thrown into deep reconsideration of her way of life. She felt that the illness had brought her to a crisis in her life which she could have faced years before. She then decided to come to this country for an analysis. Despite the extremely successful career, in which she had just been swept along, she had always nursed a longing to be a psycho-therapist or a psycho-analyst. She entered into analysis not so much because of the depression, which she felt able to handle for herself, but because she had wanted to find out about this crisis in her life that she did not understand. After a few months' analysis it began to become much clearer in relation to her developmental history – and at this time she produced three very interesting dreams.

The first dream took place the night after she had received a letter about some work she had done on an important political committee in her native country. She dreamed that *the Chairman of her committee was inviting her, quite urgently, to come up on the roof of a tall building, handing her a Sten gun saying that she must come up and fight. But when she got up to the roof she saw another tall building, with people also on its roof, also armed with Sten Guns. Although she was not particularly frightened, when she noticed that among those other people were some of her friends, she absolutely refused, threw away the gun and climbed down.* This was on a Friday. Over the weekend she had further dreams.

In the second dream *she seemed to be in some sort of a cylindrical something or other that could have been a tent or a space ship. Anyway it seemed to be cylindrical and it seemed to have been so terrifically buffeted by the wind that its outer covering was in absolute shreds. But she noticed that there was also an inner covering which she could clip together to make the structure intact again.*

The companion dream to this was that *she went to a little cobbler's shop, a really old fashioned shop with everything all "higgledy piggledy", owned by a fairly middle-aged or old man. She had gone there to have a tiny little gramophone repaired: she was not quite sure if it was a gramophone, or a pair of scales such as one can see in shops. Anyway the old man seemed to take it to pieces and to take out some odd little things, like cartridge fuses, showed her how to clip these back into place, and gave her back the tiny little gramophone – "an old-fashioned gramophone", she said, "You know, like HMV" (His Master's Voice).* She awoke feeling very contented.

Certain links between the dreams stand forth: the Sten gun, with its cartridges, links with the cartridges of the little fuse box; the blow of her illness, which is represented as the shredding caused by the blowing of the wind against the covering of the space ship that was just carrying her along, makes a further link with the word "clip", used in the sense of clipping together – but in another

45

sense it is the "clip" holding the cartridges of the Sten gun – and the clip holding the cartridge fuses in place.

Taken in series the dreams show the crisis in her life to which she had been carried from the age of thirteen by the politically adaptive superficial social "covering" of her personality. The dream showed her the aggressiveness of her political behaviour, that is its aggressive meaning for herself. This had "blown her fuse" plummeting her into the depression and was also a climb down from her successful career. But at the same time she discovered, in the "old fashioned" and "higgledy-piggledy" process of analysis, a new constructive use for her mental capacity for thinking (fuses instead of bullets, clipping together instead of clips of intellectual ammunition) through recovery of dependence on her internal object (HMV) to which she had not, presumably, listened since childhood. The link of thinking and judgment is implied in the equivocation "little gramophone or shop scales".

I would agree with Bion that dreaming *is* thinking, that dream life can be viewed as a place to which we can go in our sleep, when we can turn our attention fully to this internal world. The creative process of dreaming generates the meaning that can then be deployed to life and relationships in the outside world. This means, in a sense, that all of our external relationships have a certain transference quality, that they derive meaning from what exists in our internal world. Sometimes they derive an adult meaning so that through our identification with our internal objects the adult part of our personality is able to meet other people on an adult level through communal phantasy, a kind of congruence of internal objects. It is this congruence of internal objects that brings people together and it is living in different worlds that drives them apart so that they cannot communicate with one another.

The outcome of Bion's modification of Klein's modification of Freud's model-of-the-mind, is a view of mental functions that gives emotionality its correct place. Our passions *are* the meaning of our intimate relations, and our other relationships at the contractual and casual levels really contribute nothing to our growth and development. It is only in our intimate relationships where our passions are engaged, that we can experience the conflict of emotional meaning which nourishes the growth of the mind. Dreams of the above sort demonstrate how our problems are spelled out and worked through and solved. In analysis what we are doing, more or less, is monitoring this internal world. We monitor it through the transference, and through the dreams, and through the play of children. In trying also to give a verbal form, a verbal representation, to the thoughts that are there in the dreams or in the child's play or in the transference reactions, we make them also available for more sophisticated forms of investigation, reality testing and logical consistency. But it is the poetry of the dream that catches and gives formal representation to the passions which *are* the meaning of our experience so that they may be operated upon by reason.

In tracing the implicit and explicit models-of-the-mind utilized in clinical work by these three masters, our central thesis has been that the three models of the mind, the neurophysiological one of Freud, the geographic-theological one of Klein and the epistemological one of Bion, can be seen to link with one another to form a continuous line of development. This line develops a vision of an apparatus for mental life which embraces meaning and emotion, where understanding is transformed into personality structure, allowing for a limitless area of discourse concerning an infinitely variable non-causal system with a potential capability for growth beyond the scope of Darwinian evolutionary modes.

PART B

A REVISED THEORY OF
DREAM-LIFE

IV

Dreaming as Unconscious Thinking

In framing a theory of dreams that rests firmly on Freud's clinical use of dreams in psycho-analysis but which grows organically out of the Structural-Phenomenological rather than Topographical-Neurophysiological model-of-the-mind, it is necessary to establish our vocabulary for describing dreams. This vocabulary must be truly meta-psychological (in its extended sense, including the geographical dimension of Klein and the epistemological dimension of Bion, in addition to Freud's original four-part definition). The most lucid sequence would seem to require the definition of the dream-process as one of thinking about emotional experiences, after which the way would be clear to examine what Freud calls the "considerations of representability" (by which we will mean symbol formation and the interplay of visual and linguistic symbolic forms) and the "dream work" (by which we will mean the phantasy operations and the thought processes by which the emotional conflicts and problems seek resolution).

In order to carry through this first task I have chosen to turn to an unusual type of clinical material which we had the pleasure of hearing and discussing at a seminar for child-analysts and psychotherapists in Paris in the Spring of 1980. It relates to an extraordinary infant-observation carried out by a therapist in a municipal nursery for the children of working mothers. This observation started when the child, Matthieu, was seven months old and, because of great concern for his unsatisfactory development, metamorphosed into a three-times per week therapy by the time he was one year of age. Because the child's activities were almost entirely pre-verbal, even at the age of 23 months when the sessions now to be presented occurred, and because his understanding of language was still rudimentary, with the therapist's interpretive interventions also largely non-verbal, the whole process had a very striking resemblance to dream-content. It will be seen to illustrate phantasy and thought in action in a dramatic way that illuminates Bion's concept of alpha-function performed by the mother in the earliest mother-baby relationship.

In the sessions in question the child was presented with a new and "amazing" experience with the therapist by virtue of of a "breach" in her established technique whereby she undertook a maternal *service* to the child, namely wiping his nose, instead of confining herself to observation, thought and interpretive counter-play. Their interaction following this incident of nose-wiping will be presented as an example of infant-mother communication at a preverbal level which illustrates on the one hand Bion's thesis of the mother's role in promoting thought in the child (alpha-function) while at the same time allowing us to treat the therapist's communication to the seminar as if it were identical, or at least analogous, to a patient in analysis presenting a dream. In this context the participants of the seminar, mainly in the persons of Martha Harris and the author, will be seen to play the role of analyst, that is, sharing the experience through imagination with the therapist and helping her to discover the meaning that it had for her, not only the meaning of Matthieu's behaviour but of her own as well.

Of course it will be seen that the seminar "analysts" do not in fact, any more than do analysts in their consulting rooms, confine themselves to the mere transformation of the visual image communicated by the therapist's account into verbal form in order to define the *meaning* of the scene; they also, on the basis of experience and conceptual framework, make comments which attempt to explore the *significance* of the interaction and the mental states they portray. This division between *transforming* the expression (the symbolic form) and *discerning* the significance of the meaning thus transformed, is in keeping with Freud's original description of his method (see "The Dream of Irma's Injection") and will be further explored in later chapters on method of dream analysis. But here we have a more basic task of establishing that *the dreamer is the thinker* and the analyst is *the comprehender of his thought*. By communicating his dream in whatever symbolic form is most available to him, action, play, pictorial or verbal – perhaps a capable musician might do it musically – the dreamer enlists the aid of the analyst to transform the evocative descriptive language into the verbal language of the description of meaning, the first move towards abstraction and sophistication. By this means the thoughts are placed in a form where *thinking* in Bion's sense can commence, that is the manipulation of thoughts by processes of reason. This latter would include thinking about the processes of thought itself – thinking about thinking.

I shall come back to these issues in subsequent discussion. It will be noted that the wandering and repetitive course of the seminar has been presented verbatim for the sake of illustrating *processes.*

Matthieu was the second-born of fraternal twins, having a sister Mathilde who outweighed him by half a kilo at birth. Because of his small size (1.9 kilos) he was kept in an incubator while his mother took Mathilde home after the first eight days. The mother, who seemed an anxious woman, had been able to become fertile only after gynaecological treatment. She was overwhelmed to have two infants to care for and placed them in the day-nursery at three months to return to work. While Mathilde was an active, thriving baby, Matthieu was a cause of great concern to the nurses because of his listlessness, marked show of anxiety when approached, lack of zest in feeding, tension and sweating, inability to grasp objects, and later on to sit up or cry. His only spontaneous movement seemed to be at times a scratching movement with his finger tips. Medical examinations and even a neurological study with EEG were carried out with negative results. His behaviour at home was reported to be the same.

After five months of observation, from seven to twelve months of age, the therapist received permission from the mother to attempt a therapy, which she conducted along strictly psycho-analytical lines, employing a few simple toys which she brought with her each session in a plastic bag. Martha Harris and I first heard her observations when the child was eleven months old and then on two occasions in supervision at fifteen and nineteen months, so that by the time of the current seminar, we were fairly well-acquainted with Matthieu's remarkable progress and the therapist's equally remarkable capacity to observe and respond to him. By fifteen months he was already exhibiting a range of intense emotions with her, clearly showing strong introjective capacities in his play with her and the toys, and had even held the contact vibrantly over the summer break during which he had made striking progress in his motility and relationship to his sister and mother. It became clear in his demeanour that the therapist held a very particular role in his life, manifest by a somewhat tyrannical possessiveness towards her. But he seemed also to recognize that there were functions she did *not* perform, as for instance those related to his toilet training which, by the time of these following observations, had been started mainly by the nursery attendants.

Therapist: I will speak a little about the sessions following the Easter break; and then I will give you in detail the last session in April.

In the sessions at the beginning of March, Matthieu takes up a very particular attitude, just after my shutting the door of the little play-room. He stands completely amazed, bewildered, in front of me. When I pass behind him and sit down he keeps his body turned towards the door and turns his head towards me. He main-

53

tains this posture for about ten minutes. In later sessions he will turn his body rather more towards me, but without daring to move his feet. It is at that period that he begins to call for his mother at the beginning of the session. Later he reproduces with his own hand the movement of my hand shutting the door – and this is done in the direction of the door.

Donald Meltzer: This seems to be an illustration of Matthieu's feeling that something is splitting him. In analytic work it is of great importance, with regard to the splitting processes, to determine whether the process is experienced as active or passive in order to assess its developmental versus its pathological significance for the person. Splitting processes seem to involve both splitting of object and splitting of self, and whether it is active or passive determines which is split first, that is whether the object is split, resulting in a split of the self, or whether the self is split producing a splitting of the object.

Melanie Klein, when she first described splitting processes, and particularly splitting and idealization, maintained that they have either developmental or pathological significance depending on the degree of gentleness versus sadism with which they are motivated. But it seems to me that the recognition of passive splitting, by Bion in particular, is a much more recent development, and that it has not yet been clearly described in the literature. I have recognized this mainly in patients who have experienced it because of an actual split in their objects in early infancy – as, for instance, between mother and grandmother, mother and nurse, mother and aunt, and so on. It seems to me that when splitting has its origins in that sort of division, it is experienced as a passive process and tends to have pathological significance. On the other hand it can also be experienced passively, generally pathologically, where it has been induced by a somewhat premature disciplinary kind of behaviour on the part of the mother, particularly, for instance, in very early toilet training. In England and America a paediatric system called the Truby King method was in vogue following World War I. This paediatrician advised extremely early toilet training, starting at a few months of age, before the baby could really even sit up. He suggested that the baby should be put on the mother's lap and put on the pot, and even little suppositories used, and so on, to induce automatic toilet training. One of the effects that it can produce is not only automatic obedience but also automatic disobedience. But this facet of automatic obedience seems to be related to an extremely persecutory type of splitting and idealization. It is so primitive in its phantasy basis that it seems to have more relationship to group life, that is to group psychology, in terms of Bion's concepts of basic assumption groups and their relationships to psycho-somatic disorders.

It strikes me that this material about Matthieu revolves around his recognition that there are things the therapist does for him that are unique, and that there are also things she does not do for him. This has the effect of his feeling split between her and his mother, passively.

Martha Harris: I am wondering whether, in addition to that, or even as a prior basis on which this is superimposed, there is a development in him as the result of the attention being paid to him by the observer; it may be that the relationship with the mother has deepened thereby. He may experience her as being more interested in him and more attentive to him than hitherto, so that after the holiday there arises a conflict of loyalty because he suddenly experiences two Mummies in his life. Later there is also a Daddy who seems to be somebody more personal, someone who pays attention to him. We already saw, after the first long summer holiday when we were so amazed that he continued to develop so well, that he seemed to be able to use the experience with the therapist in his relationship with his mother and sister.

D.M.: You might say that in so far as the Oedipal tendencies of a small child have their foundations in his incapacity to share his object, he does also tend to assume that the objects would be unable to share him, and that therefore he has to make one good and one bad; to turn to the one, and to turn away from the other.

M.H.: And therefore one might imagine, had he been a little boy who had been brought to therapy by his mother, that at this point, instead of just standing immobile in the middle of the room and looking at the door, he would be calling out, hanging on to his Mummy's skirt and not wanting to come into the therapist's room. But of course Mummy is not just outside the door – it is the nursery that is outside the door.

Therapist: In the first session after the Easter break Matthieu gives me the impression of being happy and lively. At the beginning of the session he hands me the plastic bag in which the toys are kept, looking joyful; but immediately after the bag is put on my lap, Matthieu becomes a little sad and shouts "Mama!".

The next day is the beginning of a period when Matthieu calls for his father with anxiety. I go and fetch him on the terrace; he seizes my hand, without looking at me, and he squeezes my finger hard saying, "Daddy!" In the little room he does not let go of my finger; he squeezes it and puts one of his fingers in the crack of the door which is shut. He plays with my buttons, my earrings, with the dolls; he throws the toys towards the door and the window. But then, after putting the whole family of dolls along the wall he sticks his bottom just above them and begins to cry and shout desperately, "Daddy! Daddy!"

D.M.: You can see Matthieu operating at the part-object level with all these things – your fingers, buttons, earrings representing the Daddy-items of the mother's body. But the impression is that he is also experiencing it, not only as the external situation but as the internal situation as well, and that this throwing of the toys towards the doors and windows has the significance of throwing these objects, these maternal part-objects, out of his bottom and inviting his Daddy to enter into him and to take possession of his internal world. You could imagine the dream of an adult patient calling to someone out in the back garden to come in and to help him repel these invaders at the front door (that is, to invite a paternal object into his anus to aid in repelling a maternal object from his mouth).

There is a period in the analysis of Richard, in *The Narrative of a Child Analysis* in which he does a lot of biting of the pencil while Mrs Klein is talking. At the same time he shows a great tendency to have tummy aches and things of that sort during the session, so that we see that the external relationship with the analyst is so intensely internalized that he immediately experiences it as a struggle that takes place actually inside his body.

M.H.: There is also some significance in the fact that, on his return, when he has to come back to the nursery with all those other children present, this becomes very quickly internalized and felt as all those babies inside who have to be expelled and destroyed. There is some indication from this material also that he seems to be a child who has a very strong feminine capacity to take in and to hold and to think about his experiences, as we saw in earlier material which brought out his identification with the therapist in her role of observer.

Therapist: After Matthieu shouts "Daddy" he stops when I give him the big bag into which he can put the different toys. He puts his finger on the end of the handle of the little car. I put one of my fingers at the other end and move it forward a little. Matthieu smiles.

D.M.: Have you any idea why you did that? You are always doing things and we have to figure out later why you did them. You do seem to do things that have some interpretative significance and we have to work out what your interpretation was. Of course this is what intuitive people always do in playing with very small children; they initiate and respond to play in a way that puts meaning into it. One would have to assume in this context that it has something to do with initiating a play of sharing Daddy's penis: "Now Matthieu has Daddy's penis, and now Mummy has Daddy's penis", and you push it back and forth between you alternately – it is a sharing game.

M.H.: When he stuck his bottom above all those toys and shouted desperately "Daddy, Daddy", it seems to me that he felt that everything had been emptied out so that there was nothing to rescue him and he was calling for Daddy and Daddy's penis. But then, in giving him the big bag it was almost as if you were giving him more, some kind of combined Mummy/Daddy, something that could hold him and that gave him a feeling of his desperation and disorientation being caught and held so that there was then a space within which he could play. It is a bit like the desperation that a child can feel sometimes when it is held defecating into the pot, when it feels that it is losing all its good objects as well as its bad ones – its insides being quite emptied.

Therapist: Next day, immediately after my shutting the door, although he continues to squeeze my hand, he cries and shouts, "Daddy! Daddy!" I keep the plastic bag open on my lap. He continues to cry, but at the same time he manipulates another little plastic bag, very thin. He puts it first into, and then out of the big bag – as if that little bag could not be at ease either inside or outside. He makes similar movements with the little Matthieu doll.

He pulls my finger, as if he wanted to make me move. I do not know why, but I stay very firmly in my place. I feel that I must not speak; I keep silent, I just "speak" with signs: No... I will not move... I will stay there... And the longer I maintain that attitude the quieter Matthieu becomes. Whereas when I tried to speak, to "explain" as best I could what Matthieu was feeling, he became more and more anxious. Now he looks at me for the first time, silent, motionless, fixing my eyes. And I try to receive this look very firmly. He is completely relieved now, it seems to me; and he takes the thin little plastic bag, and moulds it as if he wanted to show me how soft and pliable it is.

After that there is a play of "cou-cou" behind the bed.

When I feel that he has sufficiently recovered from his crying I get up, take a paper handkerchief and clean his face; he offers no resistance. I put this handkerchief into his pocket and then I sit down again. But Matthieu, after that, looks at me completely amazed. He takes the handkerchief out of his pocket and cleans his nose again. He rubs his chin with the handkerchief, and he looks at me as if he wanted to show me that I do not care properly for him; he will show me how we ought to clean the faces of children who cry. He tears the handkerchief up and compresses it in his hand.

D.M.: You get a bit of evidence here of how close together is his emotional experience, and therefore how easily confused is his top with his bottom. Cleaning his top and cleaning his bottom are hardly distinguishable as experiences. Again we have the problem of trying to understand why you did this – why you started cleaning his face. I understand why you did not speak, and why you waited. I think I can understand that you felt that you had reached a point which was a holding position, in which you could wait for his anxiety and his conflict with you to quieten down – that is clear, and you held firm to that position. But why you responded to his "cou-cou" game by cleaning his face – that seems a bit mysterious.

M.H.: It may be the same as responding by singing him a nursery rhyme. It seems to me that at that moment talking is felt to be too abrupt, too masculine, too intrusive – it was as if you were responding to his feeling that he wanted something that would really hold, receive and, as it were, envelop him.

D.M.: The initial anxiety expressed in calling "Daddy! Daddy!" seems to have receded at the point when he started showing how flexible the little plastic bag was, and to have had the significance of his having calmed down. It suggests that he trusted you at this point, that he was saying, "You see how compliant I am. Now it is your turn to comply with me; now you are going to play a game in which you comply with me and have to seek me out all the time. Then we are going to take turns in disappearing. You disappear usually, but that is not fair, we have to take turns... I disappear and you have the anxiety and have to search for me...". But then you responded with this handkerchief business. You can imagine a more ordinary situation between a mother and child who are, say, out in the park, and the child has had a little tantrum. The mother has succeeded in calming him down and she wants to wipe his face but he immediately runs away, laughing, and wants his mother to chase him – and she catches him and cleans his face. Something equivalent has happened here. So one would have to ask the question – when did this impulse to clean his face arise? Was it before he started to play the "cou-cou" game, or did the "cou-cou" game give rise to the impulse in you? After? You are sure? Then we have to assume that the "cou-cou" game somehow gave rise to this behaviour.

M.H.: Could you say that offering the hankie, wiping his face, wiping the tears of his depression, are connected with his losing his object, the Daddy taking away his object, the door being shut? Playing hide-and-seek is playing at losing and finding his object again, because his object seeks him out and does not let him get lost.

D.M.: Maybe we should go back to what I said earlier about the splitting processes. Possibly this session is dominated by conflict between active and passive relationships with you, and wanting to take turns about passivity and activity. It might also have something to do, in the same way, with the masculine and feminine aspects of himself. They are both threatening him; there seems to be a desire for identification with each of his parents in turn. So this last piece of behaviour about the handkerchief may have the meaning of accusing you of confusing him about the differentiation between the top and the bottom of his body, as if to say, "I can deal with the top of my body; I don't need you. Your job is to clean my bottom; I can't do that myself."

M.H.: I am wondering how much he wants to be talked to rather than to have things done for him. It is not quite like an analytic situation, with interpretations by words only – you are doing this by means of actions. He is puzzling out the difference between the relationship he has with you, and the relationship he has with his mother who does not deal with or seem to notice his needs in the same way; she deals with his body.

D.M.: You may have yielded to a maternal impulse, and this is felt as confusing him, imposing some conflict of loyalty.

M.H.: He might almost be saying, "No, my mother is the one to clean me up. You are the one who is meant to look at me and to try to explain in words, even though you cannot always do it...". That very intense look might indicate that there is an expectation that you will understand something that no-one else pays any attention to. But he does seem to be a little boy who as a particularly intense need to be understood, which is remarkable, especially after having been put in the nursery at the age of three months.

D.M.: This early experience could indeed be expected to have atrophied this desire. His anxiety about his passive trends could also have been aggravated by his early experiences. The task of the splitting processes is to make a differentiation that clarifies, and therefore tends to diminish, conflict. But of course many experiments with splitting processes have the effect of aggravating conflict. For instance, if you think in terms of Bion's concept of alpha-function and the mother performing alpha-function for the child, what she does is to take the child's confusion and sort it out in a way that lends itself to splitting processes for the purpose of differentiation and the diminution of conflict.

You could think of it in a simple plastic way: when you are helping a child to do a jigsaw puzzle, and the child has just two pieces left, you might turn the pieces round so that they match the missing gaps – then the child can put them in place. But when the pieces are upside down, then he cannot make the connection. That would be equivalent to alpha-function – the turning round of the pieces.

M.H.: Coming back to his wish to be understood: many children feel the *need*, but not so much the desire, for they are so used to the need being fulfilled that they take it for granted. As Bukhovsky said, "We in the West take democracy and our freedoms for granted, so that we do not notice them". But a child like this, who has not had this understanding, does actively feel the *lack*, and now has the *desire* to make himself understood; and having had this relationship feels that there is now an understanding object to whom he must make things clear.

D.M.: In line with this you could illustrate another of Bion's concepts about what he terms the "Super"-Ego – the figure that presents itself as the Super Ego, but which is only interested in demonstrating its own moral superiority. Taking again the jigsaw model: an older sibling would not just turn the pieces round, he would take the pieces and put them in their place. The little child could then have a temper tantrum and the sibling would say, "You never can do anything for him, he is so unappreciative!"

This session clearly is dominated by the episode of cleaning his face, for it has taken on the significance of cleaning the child's bottom which extends to his genitals and is experienced as a masturbation.

Therapist: The last session I am reporting took place on April 29th of this year. Matthieu is at the end of the big room playing with a little girl. Mathilde comes close to me; her face is grave. Matthieu follows; he makes no aggressive movement against his sister but seizes my hand very firmly. He makes a small backward movement before entering the baby-room. He does not cry. In the little playroom he immediately takes the car containing the big plastic bag full of toys. He scrapes the car against the radiator, the wheels of the cot, and my feet, as if he wanted to discover what it is that hinders the sliding of the car against an object; the car has, in the centre of the wheel, a hub that acts as a protuberance; there are also protuberances on the objects against which he pushes the car.

He pushes the car rather violently against the different walls of the room, as if he wanted to find out the limits of its movements. I have to hold on to the car a little because we cannot make too much noise (the Director's office is near by). Matthieu acquiesces in my hand on the car, but he does not like it at all if my hand is put on the same part of the car as his own – then he says "No!"

He overturns the car and makes the handle scrape on the floor. Then he is interested in the big plastic bag. He doesn't open it, he gives it to me. He looks very happy when I keep the bag on my lap. He takes it back. He puts it on my head. He takes it back and gives it to me again, and... everything is wrong. He begins to cry, to shout in fury because time is passing and I don't understand at all what he wants me to do with that bag. If I keep it, it is wrong; if I give it to him, that is wrong; if I put it on my head, that is wrong; on the floor... opened... closed... nothing is right. He is at the climax of rage; suddenly, he urinates on the floor. His fury stops immediately. He looks a little amazed. I go with him and fetch a sponge. Nurse removes his trousers. I come back and wipe the floor. Then I take a handkerchief and clean his face. He offers no resistance. He subsequently plays with the handkerchief almost the entire session.

I put the handkerchief in his pocket. He takes it immediately and rubs the floor, next to the place where he had urinated a moment before and where I have sponged.

After that he goes to the window, cleans it with the handkerchief. He comes back in front of me and cleans his face with the handkerchief; he rubs his nose, his eyes, his nose again. After that he squeezes the handkerchief in his hand, as if he wanted to compress it, to gather the different pieces together.

Now, after his own face, it is my face that Matthieu tries to clean. He rubs my nose, my cheek, my ear, my earring (which is also a protuberance and was regarded, in a preceding session, as an equivalent of a "caca" from the nose.) Then he rubs my eyes, my glasses; but he is particularly interested in putting the handkerchief under my glasses. He rubs the inside of my hands. I think that he is going to clean the room again but instead, coming back in front of me, he squeezes the handkerchief in his hand, puts it to his mouth and pretends to eat it, he bites it. After that he tries to get me to do exactly the same thing – he wants me to bite, to swallow the handkerchief.

This series of movements is repeated a great many times.

But it is difficult for me, when he is "working" on my face, to understand if he wants to clean it, or if he wants to put dirty things, in an intrusive manner, into me. He tries, for instance, to thrust his forefinger into my mouth, rather violently. He walks to the door to clean it with the handkerchief. Then he discovers that the nail of his right forefinger can make a little noise against the right moulding of the door. He is very interested in that. He scratches his nail against the moulding and listens to the noise it makes. He is also very interested in the groove of the moulding. Now he tries to reproduce the experience he had when he scraped the hub of the car's wheel against the radiator at the beginning of the session, and to find out what it is that stops the sliding of an object.

Again he rubs my face; and he is interested in the comb in my hair – another protuberance.

He goes back to the door and he discovers then that on the left side there is a similar moulding to that on the right side. He scratches it with his left forefinger in the same way that he had with the right finger on the right side. Suddenly he draws a line with his left nail, from left to right, and from right to left, between the two points that he had scratched before.

A cleaning again of his face and of my own.

Then he sits down on the low scales. He rubs his bottom a little on it, and stretches his legs out on the floor in front of him. He gazes very intently. There is a wall on his right just behind him, but nothing on his left, so in rather an indifferent manner he puts his handkerchief on the left side of the scales and rubs it a little.

At some time during the session, I don't remember when – he gave me a little cushion. Now he comes back to me, rubs his nose, and then rubs the little cushion which I keep in my hand.

When he gives me the handkerchief he is interested to see how my hand clenches on it. When he takes the handkerchief back into his hand he is very happy to see me pretending to take the handkerchief back. He makes a movement as of retiring within himself to show me that the object really belongs to him, that I might desire it but that I have nothing.

At the end of the session he takes the handkerchief with him. He keeps it in the big room. He gets it out of his pocket and looks at it. He is sitting on a little chair. The nurse comes and puts a bib on him. She cleans the inside of his hands. And at the moment that she gives him a piece of bread Matthieu gives her the handkerchief.

M.H.: This session is preoccupied with what hinders the driving of the car, the little protuberances that stick out, that have nipple-like, or penis-like significance. Over and over again, throughout the whole session, there was a driving in or a going forward, and then there is a sudden stop. It seems that once the handkerchief has been given to him he has an object in his hand with which he can do all kinds of things that give him a feeling of mastery or power.

D.M.: It seems as if in cleaning the child's bottom and wiping down the groove between the buttocks you come up against the genitals.

M.H.: One also needs to consider the way in which he did not want your hands to touch the same spot on the car that his hand was on. I think he felt that if your hand touched the same place that he was holding, then you were taking the car from him – taking away his tool, or his penis.

D.M.: What do you make of the incident with the plastic bag, and why does it end up with his outburst of fury and urinating? This does seem almost like an ejaculation, doesn't it?

M.H.: When he had that plastic bag, which he wanted open, I wonder whether he wanted a place to put his penis. Later you say that you did not know what he was trying to do with your face, whether he was trying to clean it or put dirty things into it, and that he thrust his forefinger into your mouth as if he was looking for a place, an orifice, into which to put his penis. When he looked so amazed after his temper tantrum, and then urinated – which immediately seemed to quieten him – perhaps he was thinking "Well! I managed to put it somewhere after all – it came out, so it went in somewhere".

D.M.: Yes, I think that he has had something equivalent to an orgastic experience. There would seem to be something like the beginning of a fetishistic relationship to an object, and in that sense it is related to the sort of inadvertent actions and experiences of maternal services that generate transitional object attachments. It seems fairly clear that he has now invested this handkerchief with qualities that in fact belong to your hand in cleaning his face.

M.H.: The question is, when does something like that become a fetish? It has been used as a means of communicating something for which the child has no words and can find no other way of expressing.

D.M.: It looks as if the sensuality has overwhelmed the meaning at this point.

M.H.: He does do a lot with that handkerchief – he cleans the window, cleans his face, rubs his nose, his eyes, he gives it to you and then, at the end, when the nurse has given him a piece of bread, he gives her the handkerchief. He has endowed it with many qualities. I would have thought that before one could have any idea as to whether he was beginning to use it in a fetishistic way you would probably need to study it over a period of time. Children do make transitional objects that can be used as fetishes – but

63

they can be used as reminders of the parental objects, or as modes of communicating with them.

D.M.: Perhaps Matthieu has experienced you as incontinent – it excited him.

Later in the session the scratching of the door with his fingernail raises the question whether, in cleaning his face, you might have slightly hurt him because this incident suggests that not only has it aroused a response of an erotic sort, and given this handkerchief a fetishistic significance, but it has also mobilized a kind of sadistic eroticism. You would have to think of this as a transference experience. That is, he is experiencing with you something that has happened many, many times in his life already in the process of being cleaned, and in that sense it may have come up in the orderly development of the process and just found this particular experience through which to express itself. Or it is possible that this breach of your own technique may have pushed it forward in the transference before the foundation was laid for dealing with it.

M.H.: It seems that it has somehow given him not just the feeling of his urine being cleaned up, but of his urine being mopped up into this handkerchief/nappy from which comes some sort of power to enable him to be the nipple which feeds you as the baby. In some way it is taken as if his incontinence becomes something out of which a breast is created. He then pokes it into your mouth – and then he is able to give the handkerchief away. So that now he has become a feeder, a nipple, a breast. I am thinking now of how, towards the end of the session, he gives the handkerchief back and is interested in seeing how your hand clenches on it; he takes the handkerchief back and is very happy to see you pretending to take it back again. Then he makes a movement of retiring with it to show that the object really belongs to him and that you desire to have it because you have nothing – since he has it, this breast, this nipple. That would go along with the idea that there was something fetishistic in it.

The work of this therapist reminds one how stunned the psycho-analytic world was when Melanie Klein began working with children as young as 2½ years. I think that the reason for this was that although Freud had announced that little children had emotional conflicts, it was not recognized that they *worked* on their conflicts; they just had them, and certain mechanisms of defence were set in motion in relation to the distribution of libido and quantities of anxiety and so on. The work that Melanie Klein did with such children was, in a fundamental way, different from the work that Freud did with Little Hans, through Little Hans' father, from the conceptual point of view, since that was seen as making the unconscious conscious. When Little Hans' material got beyond the framework of Freud's theories – for instance the material relating to the riding with his little sister in the stork box – it was brushed aside as a "leg-pull".

But even Melanie Klein's work with these small children was felt to be contingent upon the child being able to speak and understand language. A lot of work has been done since then with mute children, with mute schizophrenics, but with all these patients it has always been assumed that they could understand language. There also grew up a concept of non-verbal communication, but it was not clearly distinguished from acting in the transference situation. Similarly Melanie Klein's concept of unconscious phantasy is not the same as the concept of unconscious thinking. "Unconscious phantasy", and its continuity with dreaming, assumed representations of concrete psychic realities, of transactions going on in psychic reality, in the internal world. In that way it was quite different from Freud's definition of thought as experimental action, experiments designed to solve problems and conflicts without needing recourse to action in the outside world. He writes in the paper on "The Two Principles of Mental Functioning" (SE XII, p.221), "It is probable that thinking was originally unconscious, in so far as it went beyond mere ideational presentations and was directed to the relations between impressions of objects, and it did not acquire further qualities perceptible to consciousness until it became connected with verbal residues... (thinking) is essentially an experimental kind of action."

Melanie Klein's concept of unconscious phantasy was different since it had no experimental implication to it. This differentiation between thought, which Freud considered to be absolutely bound to language and the use of language, and Klein's concept of unconscious phantasy, also goes back to Freud's ideas about what dreams were and what they were not. What Freud calls the "dream thought" he specifically says is not a manifestation of intellectual activity in the dreamer. Everything is brought from the day residue and taken into the dream as fragments of memories from thinking and rational activity during the day. He says, over and over again in the dream book, that *no* intellectual activity or manifestation of judgment or function of judgment goes on in the dreamer. And in keeping with that he insists that language appearing in the manifest dream content has all been lifted from actual speech said or heard during the day and is part of the day residue.

Melanie Klein's ideas about unconscious phantasies, and dreaming as the unconscious phantasies that go on during sleep, made a very great change in the ideas about dreaming – but it still left dreaming as something quite different from thinking because it did not have, in Freud's sense, any function of experimental action and problem solving; in her view, also, it did not have any intellectual activity of function of judgment operating in it.

This work with Matthieu bears a strong resemblance to work done with autistic children. It was assumed that these children did not understand language adequately and a great deal of the communication with them, although quite a lot of talking was done, was embodied in action and inaction. Thus much of the communication was non-verbal in its true sense.

It is not possible to listen to this material – both the description of the child's behaviour, and the therapist's behaviour – without coming to the conviction that thinking, in the sense of experimental action, is going on in both of them. Moreover, in addition they are working out problems of symbolic representation together at a non-verbal level – in the sense of pre-verbal. We in the seminar were trying to raise the communications to a verbal level in order to understand them, and to communicate about them with each other.

Psycho-analytic work with adult patients in recent years, excluding Bion's work, has moved in a very linguistic direction in keeping with developments in philosophy, and has borne rich fruit. It has not made much progress in investigating thinking or disturbances in thinking, because these functions have their origins at the pre-verbal level. This failure would appear to have it roots in a failure to differentiate between the problems of communication and the problems of thinking. Many of these developments which were thought to penetrate into problems of thinking have, in fact, only dealt with the problem of communication of thoughts and of thinking that was already in operation. In a similar way Freud made the same sort of mistake in his attitude towards emotions, when, in following Darwin's idea that emotions were essentially archaic modes of communication, he did not distinguish between the communication of feelings and the meaning of feelings. In the paper on "The Two Principles of Mental Functioning" he writes, "A new function was now allotted to motor discharge, which, under the domination of the pleasure principle, had served as a means of unburdening the mental apparatus of accretions of stimuli, and which had carried out this task by sending innervations into the interior of the body (*leading to expressive movements and the play of features and to manifestations of affect*). [my italics] Motor discharge was now employed in the appropriate alteration of reality; it was converted into *action*... (and thinking) is essentially an experimental kind of acting".

66

In thus relegating emotions to the menial task of "unburdening the psychical apparatus of accretions of stimuli" he deprived them of meaning and left them, through "expressive movements and the play of features", only a secondary function as primitive methods of communication. This attitude even expressed itself in what seems a most extraordinary theory, the James-Lange theory of emotions, which suggested that the subjective experience of emotions is the consequence of self-observation of this very behaviour; that a person is in the same position in relation to his own emotions as are other people, observing behaviour and construing emotions therefrom.

Our work with autistic children in the Research Group, Esther Bick's development of infant observation, Bion's development of a theory of thinking, can all be brought together to make a differentiation between thinking and phantasy.

One of the implications of this is that dreams are experiments; that the dreams patients bring to analysis are sometimes successful and sometimes unsuccessful – but not in the sense in which Freud meant this, for he considered that a successful dream kept the dreamer asleep and that an unsuccessful dream woke him. I would suggest the use of these terms in the sense that a successful dream solves the problem and an unsuccessful one does not.

Bion's work has as its foundation the assumption that an emotional experience exists, and that it can then be thought about if certain operations take place. Not only does he place the emotional experience prior to thoughts, but he also places thoughts prior to thinking – and describes thinking as the manipulation of thoughts. That seems to be the revolutionary step in Bion's work that has made it possible for us now to think about thinking. Before this postulation of the chronology of the emotional experience (the idea that thoughts could be generated from it and that thinking could be done with these thoughts) it was not possible to think about thinking. Having made that step in arranging the chronology, Bion was able to make the next step by applying Melanie Klein's discoveries (particularly the discovery of projective identification and splitting processes) to discrete mental functions themselves, not only to mental structures as she had done. These two things – the chronology of thinking processes and the application of the schizoid mechanisms to discrete mental functions – is the foundation upon which all Bion's work has been built.

One of the great difficulties in understanding Bion's work lies in being able to conceive in your mind the splitting off and the projecting of isolated mental functions. But it becomes easier if we remember that in describing the fundamental thing, the emotional experience, the word "emotional" is put right in the centre.

67

For it is in the emotion that the possibility of a meaning being extracted from this experience resides. His next step was to reconceptualize the infant/mother relationship on this basis. Under Melanie Klein's model – and this was not at all explicit but only implicit – the mother's functions for the baby were primarily of two sorts; one was services which the baby could not perform for itself: the other was the modulation of the infant's mental pain. It was assumed that so long as the baby's mental pain was kept within tolerable limits its mental development would unfold; that its development was, in a sense, a kind of biologically programmed sequence of events in the mental sphere just as it was in the bodily sphere. In this sense Melanie Klein's developmental concepts are not fundamentally different from the Freud/Abraham concepts regarding the sequence in the development of the erogenous zones. It is true that it places them in a different, more meaningful context in the internal world and makes them more concrete. However, as far as the developmental processes themselves are concerned, they are biologically determined rather than being dictated by *logical necessity*. Bion's ideas about the development of the mind are substantially different; it is, in that sense, a very *epistemological* theory – the mind is seen to develop on the basis of the acquisition of knowledge, knowledge about itself and knowledge about its objects, internal and external. You might say that, in Bion's view, the developmental process extrapolates towards wisdom, from ignorance to wisdom, whereas Klein's concept of development sees the mind as evolving from disintegration to integration – a very structural concept. Freud's concept of development, on the other hand, is primarily a psycho-sexual one that sees a migration of erogenous zones from the mouth to the genitals. Even though others, like Erik Erikson, have given it a more rounded form by talking about zones and modes of relationship, it remains the same thing; a general movement from orality and the modes of relationship that are possible on an oral basis, to genitality and the modes of relationship that are possible on a genital basis.

It seems to me that this history of psycho-analytic thought may all be accepted as substantially correct. The Freud/Abraham description of events does in fact take place, and Klein's superimpositions upon it do also happen. And what Bion has further erected on this foundation occurs also. However, Bion's description of the mind's development attributes to the mother/baby relationship a complexity that is partially absent from Klein's work and is totally absent from the Freud/Abraham conception.

You might say that, at these three different levels of the development of ideas in psycho-analysis, psycho-pathology is conceived by Freud as the consequence of *traumatic* experience; by Klein it is seen as the result of parental failure to modulate the baby's mental pain; Bion has envisaged something much more complicated, namely a relationship between the mother and baby in which the mother really does have to perform *mental functions* for the baby so that the baby may, by gradual introjection of these functions *into its internal objects,* learn to perform these functions eventually *within itself.*

The material about Matthieu gives a perfect example of what Bion has been teaching us if we consider that the nodal point of this material is where the child is "amazed" when the therapist cleans his face. What she has translated into English as "amazed" is really a perfect description – it is the perfect word for what Bion means by the emotional experience before it has been worked upon by alpha-function. The same word is used in the translation of the Hebrew in the Jewish Book of Law. It says, "Stand close to the dying because when the soul sees the abyss it is amazed." That is, it envisages death as an unbearably *new* experience – the soul has never known anything like it before. This seems to me to be the idea behind Bion's description of the emotional experience in so far as a particular emotion has never been experienced before and so does not immediately yield its meaning. It has to be worked upon to discover its meaning. But first a container must be found to hold the experience.

I do not mean that Matthieu had never had this kind of emotional experience before – but he had never had it with a person who could help him to think about it, to contain it for him. And if we observe the sequence of events that went on in the April 29th session, we see alpha-function in operation; we see the therapist trying to contain Matthieu's projection of the experience and to perform alpha-function for him. That sequence of events in which Matthieu seems to propose different configurations to her, is a way of attempting to get her to perform the alpha-function for him, to put this experience, by which he has been amazed, into a configuration or form that he can think about – for instance the sequence with the bag of toys in which he put it here and he put it there and put it on her head, finally becoming more and more frantic until at last he burst out weeping, and then urinated and was amazed again. I do not think that we can escape the impression that it is a scene that we might see repeated over and over again with any extremely young baby. Bion calls this state, in which all the fragments of potential thought cluster around an emotional experience, "the uncertainty cloud". He compares it with Pirandello's play *Six Characters in Search of an Author**. He also describes

*He does not mention one of its other sources, *The Cloud of Unknowing.*

it as the contained trying to be its own container, or searching for a container. What happened to Matthieu as it built up and culminated in his urinating, is as good a description as we shall ever get of the "uncertainty cloud", of these characters in search of an author, these fragments of incipient thought searching for a container.

Bion seems to envisage two other possibilities if these fragments of the contained do not find a container, that is if alpha-function is not performed. One is for the state of confusion to go into the body and manifest itself as a disturbance of bodily function; this he calls "the body thinking". This stands in contrast to the ability to dream and it resembles Freud's view of emotions under the pleasure principle. The other possibility is for the incipient thought to be transformed into social participation of a non-thinking sort, that is participation in the basic assumption group, the non-thinking social form. This insight is our most powerful glimpse into the potential violence in the basic assumption groups. If we are at all correct in thinking that Matthieu's urinating had an orgastic significance, so too does the eruption of violence in a group and that is why group violence so often has the distinct emotional atmosphere of sexual perversion.

V

Symbol, Sign, Epitome, Quintessence

The models of the mind with which analysts work in their consulting rooms may be as various as the individuals who practise this
method, but surely the great division is defined by the basic stuff
with which they imagine themselves to deal, whether it is psychic
energy or meaning. This cleavage naturally leads practitioners
either towards the natural sciences for their metaphors, or towards theology and philosophy as embodied in myth and literature. Freud can clearly be seen to have been divided in his approach, using one for his theories and another for the description
of clinical phenomena. In a certain sense the same could be said
of the usage of Bion, where one type of metaphor is derived from
mathematics and chemistry, and another set taken from mythology. But in Bion's case there is no cleavage in the underlying model
of the mind, only in the form of exposition. What he has borrowed
from mathematics or chemistry are modes of thought for dealing
with the model of the mind that he constructed over a period of
twenty years, a model dedicated to bringing within the purview of
the psycho-analytical method those disturbances of thought which
bulk so large in schizophrenia, but which now, with the help of his
schema, can be detected in lesser forms in less disturbed patients,
including of course ourselves in the consulting room.

This chapter is devoted to tracing the implications of Bion's
model of the mind for our understanding of symbol formation
and its various defects as we meet them in the ordinary practice of
analysis, where "ordinary" is taken to mean those patients whom
we undertake to treat with some reasonable hope of benefit. For
some people this may even include schizophrenia, patients with
organic disorders, or psycho-somatic illnesses. His model, in brief,
is as follows: the sense impressions of emotional experiences must
be worked upon by an apparatus derived by introjective identification with the primal object (maternal breast) which can organize
these impressions into (unobservable) alpha-elements from which
dream thoughts can be constructed; the linking together of alpha-
elements is accomplished by a dynamic factor (love, hate or knowing; L, H, K) operating within a mechanism composed of Ps ↔ D
(paranoid-schizoid and depressive positions plus selected fact, the

positions taken in the structural rather than economic sense) and container-contained (♀♂). These same mechanisms and dynamisms can also operate on dream thoughts to enable them to grow in complexity, level of abstraction and sophistication, and fit them for various uses and combinations. This organization of thought Bion has laid out on the model of the Periodic Table of chemical elements, as the Grid of the *Elements of Psycho-analysis* (meaning the elements of "thinking about emotional experiences"). This includes of course the possibility of thinking about thinking about emotional experiences, that is investigation of the psycho-analytical method. The Grid has been constructed, by analogy (perhaps imperfect), with the dimensions of atomic weight and valency, on the axes of "use" and "genesis" of thoughts, each axis having a certain degree of internal logic.

It is of importance to note that Bion has proposed a "mythical" apparatus to which he has invited other analysts to contribute clinical "meaning" in order that its utility might eventually be determined in practice. This model has imposed itself on my thinking about clinical phenomena, though I confess that I have never used it for "meditative review" or the "psycho-analytic game". One aspect of it, however, that remained incomprehensible to me until recently was Bion's attempt to imagine how such an apparatus of thinking could come into existence in the individual (or in the species). Let me quote his poetic description lest its emotionality and beauty be lost in translation into my prose.

(Elements of Psycho-analysis, p.39) "It is tempting to suppose that the transformation of beta-elements to alpha-elements depends on container-contained and the operation of paranoid-schizoid and depressive position (Ps ↔ D) depends on the prior operation of container-contained. Unfortunately this relatively simple solution does not adequately explain events in the consulting room; before container-contained can operate, container has to be found and the discovery of container depends on the operation of Ps ↔ D. It is obvious that to consider which of the two, container-contained or Ps ↔ D, is prior distracts from the main problem. I shall suppose the existence of a mixed state in which the patient is persecuted by feelings of depression and depressed by feelings of persecution. These feelings are indistinguishable from bodily sensations and what might, in the light of later capacity for discrimination, be described as things-in-themselves. In short beta-elements are objects compounded of things-in-themselves, feelings of depression, persecution and guilt and therefore aspects of personality linked by a sense of catastrophe;... The beta-elements are dispersed; this dispersal should be terminated by Ps ↔ D and a selected fact unless the patient seeks a container that compels

cohesion of the beta-elements to form the contained. The dispersed beta-elements, in so far as they seek the container, may be regarded as an abortive prototype of a container, a container loosely structured like the reticulum of Dr Jacques. They may equally be regarded as the abortive prototype of the contained, a loosely structured contained before compression to enter the container.... If the dispersed beta-elements find no container (the model corresponding to container is presumably the breast) the dispersed beta-elements, functioning as we have seen as a loosely-knit reticulum (contained in search of a container) become, as it were, far more actively depressed-persecuted and greedy. (p.42)... The mechanisms involved in these primitive phenomena can be regarded, at their simplest, as Ps ←→ D (or fragmentation ←→ integration) and container-contained (or expulsion ←→ ingestion).... Ps may be regarded as a cloud of particles capable of coming together, and D as an object capable of becoming fragmented and dispersed. Ps, the particles, may be regarded as an uncertainty cloud. These elementary particles may be regarded as closing on to one elementary particle, object or beta-element, a process that is a particular instance of the general movement represented by Ps ←→ D."

Before going on to our main discourse, having introduced its background in Bion's model of the mind as an apparatus for thinking about emotional experience, let me add another preamble: Hamlet is asking Guildenstern to play upon a recorder:

Guildenstern	I know no touch of it, my lord.
Hamlet	'Tis as easy as lying: govern these ventages with your finger and thumb, give it breath with your mouth, and it will discourse most eloquent music. Look you, these are the stops.
Guildenstern	But these cannot I command to any utterance of harmony; I have not the skill.
Hamlet	Why, look you now, how unworthy a thing you make of me! You would play upon me; you would seem to know my stops; you would pluck out the heart of my mystery; you would sound me from my lowest note to the top of my compass; and there is much music, excellent voice, in this little organ; yet cannot you make it speak. 'Sblood, do you think I am easier to be play'd on than a pipe? Call me what instrument you will, though you can fret me, you cannot play upon me.

Enter Polonius

God bless you, sir!

Polonius	My lord, the Queen would speak with you, and presently.
Hamlet	Do you see yonder cloud that's almost in shape of a camel?
Polonius	By th' mass and 'tis like a camel, indeed.
Hamlet	Methinks it is like a weasel.
Polonius	It is back'd like a weasel.
Hamlet	Or like a whale?
Polonius	Very like a whale.
Hamlet	Then I will come to my mother by and by.

The question that arises from this interchange is this: why is it that a pipe is not a suitable symbol for Hamlet, nor a cloud for Rosencrantz, Guildenstern and Polonius, while a weasel, camel and whale do have the requirements to symbolize the three? The answer to such a question, in terms referrable to Bion's model, would have to satisfy several requirements. It would need to define the sense impressions of the emotional experience which were being worked upon, the selected fact that was being used to harmonize the disparate elements of the uncertainty cloud, and the evidence that Ps had been transformed into D (disintegration transformed into integration) to form the alpha-element, or symbol which can be linked together (under the dynamism of L, H, or K) to form a narrative, the dream thought. In equating alpha-element and symbol I am following Bion's suggestion that alpha-elements are themselves unobservable.

The point is that the pipe cannot symbolize Hamlet, and is therefore an inadequate symbol for narrative linkage in Guildenstern's thought about how to deal with Hamlet because it has no "heart of mystery". The cloud cannot serve as a symbol for Rosencrantz, Guildenstern and Polonius because its form is ever-changing and insubstantial. But camels, weasels and whales can symbolize the three because their behaviour is seen by Hamlet as sub-human, the pompous Rosencrantz, the sly Guildenstern and the blown-up Polonius who speaks for the Queen forgetting she is Hamlet's mother. If Guildenstern is weaselish, weasels must also be seen as Guildensternish. What is implied in this? This is not a "symbolic equation", to use Hannah Segal's term. That would be the basis for a notational system, a hieroglyph; like a coat of arms, weasel "stands for" Guildenstern. But a symbol is not a sign, it is a device for trafficking in meaning, a device for linking which expresses a congruence but implies an increment of meaning to both terms.

By saying that Guildenstern is "like" a weasel, or is weaselish, Hamlet would imply that his behaviour is subhuman, without ethic or values. But he would also imply that weasels are like courtiers, slaves to the monarchy of their appetites, different from other beasts of prey, say the lion. A sign may derive its utility by capturing a quintessence of form or function or simply may be agreed upon, conventionally, for the sake of communication, as in a phonetic alphabet. Or a sign may garner its meaning from a class of which it is the epitome, as a sword may be the sign for the class of all possible weapons. The recorder is not sufficiently congruent in its functions with Hamlet to serve as a symbol in its link to him. A cloud is not congruent enough in its form to serve as a symbol for camels, weasels or whales.

Let us now turn back to Bion's description of the "uncertainty cloud" seeking a container. I shall present some clinical material derived from experience of supervision, using it to replace the example outlined by Bion of the patient who attempted to use the furniture of the consulting room as symbols for thinking, a move which the analyst found to be inadequate for its purpose but at least an advance over having to manipulate the concrete objects of the environment. This replacement cannot be taken as an observation that confirms the utility of Bion's formulation, as it is not my observation. It is merely a first-hand way of describing what I think Bion means and how I can imagine its finding realizations in the clinical setting.

A thirteen year-old boy (Albert) has been in psychotherapeutic treatment for six years, the last three of which have been with a male therapist. He is severely debilitated in his social capacities, ineducable and extremely difficult to understand, his speech being of the type often described as "scanning". His developmental arrest seems to have been the sequel to a severely autistic early childhood. The first year of his therapy was spent almost exclusively on the couch, bouncing on his knees, giggling and chattering incomprehensibly, while variously picking threads, stroking the material, pinching and nuzzling the pillows. This gradually became amplified by drawings which at first consisted of lines of ticks or other simple signs. But in the second year "businesses" began to appear in his speech, the "electricity business" and the "pylon business" in particular. Vague, rapidly drawn landscapes with pylons took shape and the pun on pylon became apparent in his behaviour and giggling on the couch, and eventually towards the therapist. During this time his initial reluctance to come and irritability towards the therapist slowly became replaced by eagerness, impatience, excitement. The summer break of 1977 seemed to impinge upon him powerfully and in the autumn term a new "business" appeared, the "silver star" business, vaguely associated with Western films. But another new phenomenon also emerged; insistent enquiry of the therapist to tell him what was "real". This was accompanied by a new tendency to look into, or at least at, the therapist's eyes and to be disturbed if the therapist looked away or covered his eyes while lost in thought about this incomprehensible material.

I suggest that this boy is in transition from a two- to a three-dimensional relation to his therapist and that the "silver star business" catches him in midstream. In narrative form, a Kleinian-Bionic myth, it would go something like this: this boy is able to relate himself to a therapist only as a sensual couch-mummy whose surface is full of electricity-excitement. But there are so many other children also piling on this mummy that no object takes shape in his experience, the meaning of which remains like an uncertainty cloud in his mind. In his search for a container of his experience he tries to use the paper but finds that the bits of sensation are undifferentiated and cannot be put in any meaningful order but only an arbitrary one (lines of ticks). In a second attempt he uses one of his senses, his eyes, to try to create an object on the paper to function as a container, but it is so compounded of his emotion (electricity), activity (pile on) and visual image (a pylon with its legs, body and arms holding the cables) that it is more like a reticulum (the web of girders and cables) than a container. It therefore fails to perform the function of communication except as an evacuation of confusion and catastrophic anxiety. But then he begins to notice that his therapist exists in the room and regularly emits certain sounds, the absence of which made him quite miserable over the summer break. He has also noticed that these sounds seem to come when two silver stars (the therapist's eyes) are visible, neither turned away nor covered by his hand while in thought. These silver-star eyes seem somehow connected with the badge on the chest of some person in Western films, associated with law and order. They are signs of law and order and would therefore be suitable as emblems of the "real", a kind of "seal of approval" to differentiate reality (psychic and internal) from delusion.

At this point in the development of the therapy the boy seems to have located an object that gives more promise than the piece of white paper of functioning as a container of his uncertainty cloud. It is felt to be a reality-detector capable of giving a "bit" of information, yes or no, it is or is not real. He is therefore at a point of using the therapist as an instrument for acquiring information which his senses cannot provide for him, like any scientist uses his instruments. But he is not yet able to use a container that can perform alpha-function. In order to perform that function it would need to have a space inside that could contain his projected "uncertainty cloud" of the "sense impressions of emotional experience". So we are probably more correct in saying that he is looking "at" rather than "into" the therapist's eyes. His silver stars are like the early astronomer-astrologer's picture of the heavens, composed of points shining from heavenly bodies like the plough, the bear, the hunter, etc. While he, the ancient, held this model of the heavens he could not use his observations to think about the heavens themselves nor about the earth's relation to the heavens; he could only use them as a tabula rasa onto which to project earthly images, which could then only have earthly relationships. But he could use their fixed relationships for navigational purposes.

In *Explorations in Autism,* particularly in the section by Doreen Weddell about Barry, an extensive description was offered of this same type of transition from two- to three-dimensionality. We did not, however, at that time link it clearly with Bion's work on thinking, and for a simple reason: we had not yet begun to understand his work nor see the immense influence it was already producing on our modes of thought and capacity for observation in the consulting room. But while the work with Barry represented a clinical discovery, this account of Albert can only claim the status of a mythic example drawn from clinical experience. It must remain to be seen whether in fact the projected pathway to three-dimensionality will be followed and whether it will result in the expected improvement in the boy's capacity for thought. We are claiming insights that we cannot corroborate. One of these, by implication, is that Albert made "pylons" rather than pictures of pylons on the paper. What do I mean? Simply this: Albert did not draw a "picture" at all, he drew a pattern, a copy of the pattern of girders and wires of a pylon not a picture of a structure called a pylon. It was, so to speak, a representation of pylonishness. But a representation is a sign, not a symbol; one cannot represent something abstract like pylonishness except by some object which is the quintessence of pylonishness. On the other hand the network of girders and cables belongs only to a certain class of pylons and is not essential to pylons, and so cannot depict the quintessence of pylonishness. Consequently it could be said that Albert was trying to create a pylon on paper to serve as a concrete thing-in-itself, thereby using the paper as a container into which he could evacuate his uncertainty cloud of an emotional experience of pylonishness, whose reality he could not determine.

We have come some distance thus far in differentiating symbols from signs of various sorts, and thus of distinguishing between the

77

paraphernalia of communication and the equipment of thought. Symbols are pieces of this latter equipment and they represent either objects of external or psychic reality, or the relationships into which they enter – the latter not to be confused with abstractions that represent relationships, for instance the signs in mathematics. The main thing about symbols, I am asserting, is that they cannot be understood simply in one direction, but must be seen to enrich both members so linked. The linkage itself must be substantial, composed of an overlap or congruence in form or function, perhaps preferably both.

Hamlet, toying with Guildenstern and Polonius, may have served as a useful entrée to Albert's difficulty in symbol formation, but what are we to make of the other convergence in those two bits of life, namely Albert's wish to have some means to distinguish what is real, and Hamlet's assertion that playing the recorder is as easy as "lying"? The *double entrendre* is apparent, for while Hamlet means something like "easy as falling off a log", he also implies "easy as telling lies". But clearly there is a discontinuity between his disingenuous description of the technique of playing the recorder ("govern these ventages" etc.) and the actual difficulty of learning to play the instrument. By saying that it is as "easy as lying" he is also demonstrating how easy it is to lie, and thus, by implication, how hard it is to tell the truth. But a child might see someone play the recorder and seize it eagerly to "govern its ventages" in full expectation of music emerging. It would not be a matter of lying but a simple failure of imagination if the child, in asking for the instrument, asserted that he could play it. In so far as lying is a mis-representation of the truth, it is essential that the truth be known and further that its correct representation be also known. Clearly, the ease of lying is not the ease of impoverished imagination or its near neighbour, confabulation; the ease of lying must not reside in the knowing of the truth but in the saying of it in a misrepresentational form. This must be just as true of internal communication between parts of the self and with objects, as it is true of external communication.

Does our study of Hamlet and Albert in fact carry us in the direction of exposing the internal structure of lies? Clearly we cannot ascribe to them simply the quality of containing mis-information of the moon-is-made-of-green-cheese variety. That might be a lie in the mouth of an older child talking to a younger one, but it could never be a lie in the mouth of a returning astronaut. Why? Why cannot Hamlet be played upon by Guildenstern nor overawed by Polonius? Clearly because they are not close enough to the truth to gain credence. And how does that link with Hitler's discovery of the power of the big lie, only a small percentage of which has to be lent credence to accomplish its task? I am suggesting that the credibility of a lie depends not on its quantitative relation to the truth but its structural congruence or functional congruence, like symbols. That is, a lie must mis-represent the truth by employing pseudo-symbols (Hamlet's cloud). Once the symbolization is acquiesced in, the acquiescence in the relationships depicted is implied. Hitler's representation of the Jews as rats, the racist's representation of the coloured man as sub-human, the farmer's classification of vermin, all imply values and consequently actions. The problem of detecting lies resides in just this subtle area, of detecting the congruence of the items of the symbolic linkage. The pipe does not have Hamlet's "heart of mystery", the cloud is essentially formless and is thus as unrelated symbolically to camels and weasels as the Queen is to Hamlet's mother. They do not merely belong to different systems but have incongruent positions in their respective systems. The "heart of mystery" in Hamlet exists in his will, capacity for decision, and incapacity to employ his capacity. The recorder has no such mystery; that has its being in the music, not the instrument. Similarly the system in which Gertrude is the Queen and exercises power derived from many sources is quite different from the system in which she is Hamlet's mother and has abandoned her power derived from her relationship to his father. The Queen is a ritual and political role; the mother is an intimate relationship. They cannot stand for Hamlet in a symbolic relationship to one another, as they might for many people, because they have too little functional congruence in his mind.

Let us examine another clinical vignette also derived from supervision. The therapist has been treating a seven year old who had a moderate autistic start in life from which he is now recovering after three years of treatment, the first two having been with a different young woman. Charles's bizarre behaviour has nearly ceased and his relative mutism has given way to argumentativeness in which an astonishing skill in deviousness has revealed inself in the interest of extracting from the therapist a promise not to "feed other babies". His attacks on her for refusing to submit have the meaning of destroying the integrity of the breast, producing the "volcano breast" which he depicts in drawing and model as an object of perverse excitement and mystification. In his persuasiveness he presents a convoluted use of language reminiscent of the "dervishing" characteristic of his previous withdrawn states. When his logic is refuted or his cajoling resisted, obscenity and spitting burst forth. One way of representing his attack is to crack the holder of the felt pen, extract the coloured felt and use it for drawing, arguing that since its function has been preserved, the is a "felt-tip pen" and that therefore no essential act of destruction has taken place. It is necessary for the therapist to demonstrate that the function has not been preserved, as evidenced by the stain on his fingers and the poor quality of his drawing. Spitting ensues. The logic is that of an inquisitor who argues that the burning of the heretic in fact preserves his immortal soul and drives out the satanic demon who has possessed him through his irrelevant body.

If we take it that the felt tip represents the nipple and the holder with its reservoir of dye represents the breast we may say that it is at one level a suitable symbol for the breast and nipple as combined object in so far as the mechanics of the milk flow is concerned, but since what is being represented is also the psychological function, to install objects in the inner world (the drawings), it is inadequate. The drawings would be a suitable depiction of Charles's internal situation or perhaps his faeces under certain circumstances, and the felt-tip pen might therefore represent the mechanical function of his rectum and anus. If the pen had been an instrument by means of which the therapist represented her interpretations in graphic form it could have been a suitable symbol of the breast in this relationship. And in so far as the therapist has provided the pen for his use in carrying on the therapy with her, it might represent the breast. It would thus be "her" pen and not Charles's which was being destroyed and the issue of his using it in a manner not consonant with her intentions and without her agreement would be central. In fact the debate as to the proprietorship of the toys has been a central issue for some time, with particular reference to the question of his taking home a baby doll. Was it stealing if he did so without the therapist's agreement?

It is evident that the extracting of the felt tip and the extracting of the promise not to "feed other babies" are closely linked through the phantasy of being allowed by the mother to remove the nipple from the breast. This would link with the stealing of the baby, which Charles justifies on the grounds that he can feed babies also. If analysis is accomplished by talking and is to be equated with nourishing the mind of a baby, he can talk, perhaps even out-talk the therapist. If his drawings convey meaning to her as well as talking, then his drawings may also nourish babies once the equipment is "his". Guildenstern would be begging Hamlet to give him the recorder on the grounds that he has as many fingers as Hamlet with which to "govern the ventages". This logic is adequate once the premise that the pen is a suitable symbol for the analyst's breast (mind) is accepted. But we have said that the felt-tip pen would be an adequate symbol for the mechanical structure and function of breast and nipple but not for its psychological function, in so far as the feeding situation involves a contact and commerce between mother and baby, mind-to-mind. Hamlet would not be able to complain if Guildenstern was learning to play upon him, in the manner of his training case, as he might ask for the recorder in order to learn to play upon it. That would be a situation in which the "heart of mystery" in Hamlet would be sufficiently recognized and equated with the "heart of mystery" in musical composition or interpretation. But Charles, in the service of mis-representation, has shifted his ground in his argument from the psychological to the mechanical level. His method of mis-representation could be said to have the internal structure of a paradox, employing different levels of abstraction to create an appearance of congruent relationship. (Russell).

It can readily be seen that in approaching symbol formation in the service of representing the truth, and anti-symbol formation in the service of mis-representing the truth, I am following Bion's suggestion that lies should be represented in his schema not as Column 2 but as a negative form of the entire Grid. This would allow for the possibility of lies being constructed at various levels of thought and of their being put to various uses. The example of Charles's debate about the felt-tip pen would not seem to find its point of departure from the truth at the level of alpha-function, the creation of the symbol itself, but rather at the dream-thought or mythic level in which it was being employed, first to represent a mechanical system and later a psychological system. In Grid terms it would have been elevated first to the level of abstraction which was a conception of mechanical relations (row E), but later treated as part of a scientific deductive system (Row G).

Where then have Hamlet, Albert and Charles taken us? I have tried to focus attention on symbol formation in several ways: by distinguishing it as an essential item in the equipment of thought different from various devices of notation and classification, taking these latter as paraphernalia of internal and external communication; by trying to examine the internal structure of symbolic linkages, asserting that they are the product of a creative act whose essence lies in the discernment of overlap or congruence in structure, function or both. I have suggested that it is essentially creative because the linkage enriches the meaning content of both members. This process of discovering the congruence has been construed in terms of the model suggested by Bion of the uncertainty cloud of disparate particles finding a container within which the mechanism of paranoid-schizoid and depressive positions (disintegration-integration) can organize the particles around a selected fact by means of the dynamism of either love (L) hate (H) or knowing (K) to produce either alpha-elements (symbols which can be used for linkage in narrative form as myths) or growth to higher levels of abstraction and sophistication. Bion suggests that when these elements of thought are brought together from different levels of growth so that they include sensa (alpha-elements), myth (row C), and passion (which he defines as the desire to construct a scientific deductive system), molecules of thought result which are the primary objects of psycho-analytical study. Upon this foundation for conceptualizing symbol formation as the primary move for representing, and thus for thinking about, the truth, I have tried to examine the methods for formation of pseudo- or perhaps anti-symbols while Albert's silver stars would be inadequate symbols functioning as signs. Charles's material was used to suggest the ways in which this theory of thinking could be used for detecting the internal structure of lies, where lies are taken not simply as misinformation but as mis-representation for the sake of producing mis-interpretation of the emotional experience that is being thought about.

We may now turn our attention to the difficult task of defining the element of congruence, in either form or function or both, which must bind the two sides of a symbolic relation to one another in order to establish the possibility of a creative "intercourse" between them. Bion has provided us with a tentative model for the crucible in which this wedding of elements may occur, the container-contained model, the dynamism of paranoid-schizoid and depressive positions plus selected fact, and the positive linkage of love, hate or knowing to fire the combination. It is a very chemical model indeed but it serves our present needs with its source of a particular type. I present a clinical example to serve as a base for discussion.

A man in his forties was approaching the Easter break in an atmosphere of mixed expectation and discontent, for the termination of his analysis had been tentatively set for that summer. To the early morning session on the Friday he brought four discrete dream images:

1. a newly cleared bridle-way has nonetheless three hazel saplings growing in the middle;
2. a handsome young couple are kneeling in a manger before a young tomato plant with two branches and a tomato at the end of each, sprouting from a Gro-bag;
3. in the anatomy lab his woman analyst shows him a female torso with which he wishes to have intercourse but cannot bring himself to do it;
4. he is lying on a bed when a tall thin man of 51 enters and lies across him; he is paralysed, in will, so that he cannot throw him off.

Clearly the most obvious common denominator of these images is the figure of the Crucifixion, and the most obvious emotional common denominator is paralysis of the will. But the image of Jesus and the emotional state of the patient, feeling helpless to oppose either the Easter break or the termination, both of which are linked strongly with the event of the birth of his younger sister when he was 4½ years old, are variously bound together. So we might say that the congruence of his emotional state with the image, not the emotional state, of the Crucifixion has been represented in four different ways. Can this afford us an opportunity for examining the nature of the congruence itself? Let us examine the associative background of the four images to see if this takes us any distance.

a. He is a keen walker and belongs to his local association for keeping footpaths open. The one in the dream was more like a forest road or bridle-way, and he notes the pun. Let us assume it is mummy's vagina to be kept open, free of either daddy's genitals or new babies. He notes the pun on saplings and hazel nuts.

b. He had a religious period in puberty and still flirts with rather mystical ideas of visitations from the dead (both parents are deceased). He is becoming a keen gardener as was his father, and has moved from an estranged to a close relationship to his two children during the analysis. They are similar in age difference to himself and sister.

c. He is on the verge of moving home after a period of estrangement from his wife which commenced with the birth of his daughter and in which he acted out his childhood seduction of his sister. His wantonness has recently been directed towards his more attractive women clients but has been under control. His sexuality towards his wife, long in abeyance connected with her motherliness, is slowly returning.

d. The age 51 perhaps links with his pen, a Parker 51, not much good. He is troubled by a continuing inhibition in reading and in writing, which is essential to his professional work. But he would also like to be able to write more creatively in the fields of his special (hobby) interests.

The first striking feature is that the four dream images appear to have associative reference to four different areas of his life: outdoor life and naturalist studies; religion and mysticism; domestic life and sexuality; study and creative writing. This would suggest that all four areas had been contaminated with infantile significance, and thus had been subjected to anxiety, irrational actions, irrational enthusiasms or untoward inhibitions. And it is further true that the drawing of the infantile processes into the analytic transference has clarified all four of these areas in his life. But similarly the approaching ending of of the analysis is threatening to re-establish these contaminations of his adult life – interests, activities, intimate relations, work, pleasures. Jealousy of the "new baby" seems to be the driving force and we see him struggling against a new eruption of sadistic sexuality having the meaning of killing the new baby, perhaps particularly a new baby brother. This murderousness could either be cynically disguised as protective of the mother (clearing the bridle-way), or idealized as the appreciative eating of the rival tomato-babies, or eroticized in a necromantic perversion, or disguised as an identification and inhibition.

So it might be said that we have arrayed before us four symbolic relationships, each touching upon a different facet of the emotional situation surrounding the holiday break as the penultimate of his analysis. Each facet has found a mode of representation in symbolic form and behind each such linkage we have been able to discern, quite clearly, the image of the Crucifixion. Could it therefore be said that what these four symbolic linkages have in common might reasonably be taken as an indication of the area of congruence between emotional state and symbolic representation of it. If so, the unifying image of the Crucifixion which can be discerned behind the community of symbols would represent something equivalent to a first differential in the calculus, the slope of the symbolic curve, as it were. Each symbol would seem to have its own validity in reference to the particular facet of the emotional experience which it is meant to represent and thereby enrich. The four taken together demonstrate the nature of the area of congruence and thus reveal surprisingly an indication of the creative function, how the coition of the two members of each coupling produces something that is revealing both of their meaning beyond what the linkage openly declares and at a higher level of abstraction, perhaps generalization. From any one of the four an experienced analyst facing the Easter break might have guessed the background image of the Crucifixion, but taken together the phenomenon becomes unmistakeable. They cross reference, take a "fix" on the area of congruence and reveal its content. It is an example of what Bion would call reality testing by multiplication of vertices.

I propose now to make an exercise to see if it might enrich our understanding of symbol formation to practise forming symbols to represent that process, that is first derivatives. We might even hope that such a series, like my patient's four dreams, might lend themselves to the discernment of a second derivative, and thus lead us closer to the heart of mystery while demonstrating something of the essential meaning of such concepts as "level of abstraction" by non-abstractionist methods.

Consider the colour series and colour charts, for instance: could we contrast the mixing of pigments with the multiplication of filters? Imagine the colour chart with its blue and red discs overlapping to make a purple area. Now imagine the screen on which the light from two overlapping filters has been cast, so that the red disc and the blue disc give birth to a black area where the light has passed through both filters. Could we take this to represent the process by which meanings mate in the first case, caricatured by a process of serial extraction of meaning in the second?

Consider the field of genetics: the intelligent interest of man assists animals to overcome the rigidity of their mating and group behaviour to produce new strains which will breed true. The mating of Queen Pasiphae's Zeus-inspired mad passion and the bull produced the Minotaur; the mating of critical masses of uranium generate violence and the radiation which in its turn produces monsters.

Consider the beauty of the Gloucestershire landscape where the removal of fieldstone has created at once a splendid tilth and beautiful walls, barns, cottages; compare the consequence of enclosure and the "clearances" in Scotland where the greed of absentee landlords drove the cotter into exile while the grazing of sheep and the felling of forests for charcoal to feed the steel industry of the south invited erosion, the heather and the gorse.

VI

Dream-Life: The Generative Theatre
of Meaning

We have come some distance in these preliminary chapters, having examined the historical basis for a new theory of dreams, the epistemological problem concerning the evidence of dream-life, the grounds for considering dreaming as a form of unconscious thinking equivalent to the actions and play of babies and small children, a theory of symbolism which places it at the core of the process for thinking about the meaning of our emotional experiences, and finally an outline of the theory of extended metapsychology upon whose foundation we wish to construct our theory of dreams. It is necessary now to outline the theory itself so that we may examine its various components in some greater detail.

Let us start some dream material to which we may refer back as we go along. You will recall the four "crucifixion" dreams: the cleared bridle-way, but for the hazel saplings; the young couple worshipping their tomato plant; the inhibited necrophilia; and the paralysis by Mr Parker 51. Let us add to that series another duet of dreams from a young man who returned to analysis after a weekend reporting that he had a new girl-friend who seemed very interested in him, had gone back to his flat with him but had probably been disappointed that he had made no sexual advance to her. The trouble had been that he had not yet written the lecture which he had to deliver the morning of the session to his senior colleagues, although he had known of it for over a month. Not only had he disappointed the girl but he had had to cancel a lecture to his students as well. Two little dream images were vivid in his mind from the brief nap he had had in his office after writing until five in the morning.

1. Richard Nixon, although not yet elected President, seemed to have been given full use of the White House and its facilities, which he proceeded to abuse to set up his gang.
2. Mr Callaghan, who was visiting Washington on a state visit with his family, had not even had a car put at his disposal, but all were being squeezed into a taxi.

The first patient's dreams appear to reveal something of the infantile conflicts that underlie various aspects of his adult life and his approach to the termination of the analysis: the country walker and naturalist; the religious man with mystical trends; the sexual man and his sensual greed; the creative man and his writing inhibition. In all four dreams he is keenly involved in emotional conflict. But the second patient is distanced as an observer of a state of affairs in his internal world which has interfered with his pursuing his desires and meeting his obligations; a psychopathic bit of his infantile personality is given free access to the facilities for thought (the White House, representing the breast), while his good internal family is given short shrift. Upon this internal model the apportioning of his waking life-time is determined.

We spend one third to one quarter of our lives asleep and the experiments with rapid eye-movements (REM) demonstrate that at least twenty per cent of that time is occupied with dreaming. People are clearly divided in their attitudes towards sleeping as well as towards dreaming, ranging from those who consider that part of life to be one of the great pleasures, and those who lament the loss of time that could be spent in other waking activities if only some drug could be discovered to obviate this physiological nuisance. If we take seriously Bion's suggestion that the neurophysiological apparatus has evolved a mind which can feel, think, remember, judge, decide, communicate on the basis of a model, that model being the experience of the gastro-intestinal system, it would not surprise us to find that the mind behaves like a ruminant animal. It seeks its food, ingests it and then settles down to ruminate and digest it. It would not seem too fanciful a metaphor, especially if we consider that metaphor is the method *par excellence* by which the mind operates. Bion has given us a theory of thinking which envisages this ingestion (the emotional experience) and the process of digestion (alpha-function, the Grid, Ps ⟵⟶ D, container-contained, L H and K, vertices, transformations). But of course, as he stresses, it is a relatively "empty" hypothesis, and he has left us the task of filling it with life, particularly clinical life. We must remember that the gastro-intestinal model has room in it for other possibilities: the evacuation of the indigestible as well as the potentially poisonous byproducts of digestion. If we are to construct a theory of dreams upon this model, it must allow for these three processes: digesting the experiences to make available the truth as the "food of the mind"; evacuation of the indigestible, irrelevant aspects of the emotional experiences; evacuation of the lies which are the "poison of the mind" generated as by-products in the Negative Grid.

Such a theory seems, and indeed in many respects is very different from Freud's. His view that the latent content had always to be worked upon by distortion to deceive the censorship, finds considerable similarity to the distinction between the truth which dreams struggle with and the lies that invade them to deal with the excesses of mental pain which inhabit the conflicts. And of course there is some truth in the idea that the dream is the guardian of sleep in so far as the excesses of anxiety may indeed disturb the sleeper, just as undue stimulation from inside the body or from the environment may do. But we will not wish to assign to this trivial function more than a subsidiary position in our theory. The dreams of our lecturer illustrate the very simple device of distancing by which the conflict and its attendant anxiety may be modulated in the dream process, a device surely "as easy as lying".

In a similar way Freud's idea of the day residue can also be embraced, but we need to look more deeply into the question of the selection of items from the hubbub of daily life which find expression. He noted the surprising fact that the day residues seemed often to be trivial matters, far from the conscious preoccupations and dramas of the day. Rightly he concluded that some particular link to infantile experience was necessary for a daytime event to qualify for dream representation. But that was all formulated in days long before the analytical method took firm hold of the transference as a continuous process whose systematic study could be viewed as the heart of the psycho-analytical method. Today analysts who have preferred this more immediate method to the reconstructive–retrospective one, naturally think of the infantile processes as current, on-going, uninterrupted by the waking, conscious experiences of the day. Rather the unconscious processes of dealing with the emotional experiences, that is the aspects of experience which bear significance of intimate human relationships as against the practical matters involving human or non-human objects in the outside world, would indeed appear from analytical experience to form a continuum. Susan Isaacs' "unconscious phantasy" which Melanie Klein exploited so fully and which Bion has assigned the position of Row C in his Grid (dream thought and myth) would seem a suitable concept for the description of dreaming. That is, we would consider dreaming to be as continuous in the mind as is digestion in the body, but concentrated more fully on its task when the other mental processes of dealing with the outside world are in abeyance during sleep. This supposition is strongly borne out in the consulting room by the phenomenon which some patients refer to as "flashes", sudden inexplicable, vivid visual images, seemingly unrelated to the immediate verbal exchange. When they are treated as dream images they yield a rich insight into the infantile transference active at the moment.

The intrusion of these "flashes" into the flow of talk in analysis is reminiscent of what Freud called "the body entering the conversation", the classic example being Dora playing with her reticule. Here we would say that the "dreaming process has entered the conversation" and entered it as a visual language, often as poignant as a political cartoonist's drawing worth a thousand words. And it is this extended concept of language, the diversified language of the multiplicity of symbolic forms (Cassirer, Langer, Wittgenstein, Russell) to which we must turn our attention. If we are to view dreams as a language, we must take it as one that is essentially internal, a mode of internal communication. This means that, as with verbal language, we will need to study and comprehend not only its lexicon but its grammar. I hesitate to say "syntax" for that seems to imply a more minute structuring than the problem of dreams, like that of composition in the graphic arts or music, would seem ready to reveal to us. But the grammatical structure of dreams, the way in which separate dream passages or images seem to relate logically to one another, often seems to be apparent. For instance our lecturer's dreams seem to have an "if this... then this" structure. Our Easter patient's series might lend itself to this paraphrase: "As long as A, B and C, it is no wonder that D". That is, "As long as I still want to destroy mummy's little saplings because I cannot produce little tomato plants myself and am tempted to use her body merely to satisfy my sensuality, it is no wonder that my pen lies heavy in my paralyzed hand."

But if we are to approach dreams as internal dramas to whose debates we wish access, we must be content to derive a very imperfect understanding of what is happening on the stage, whether it be the stage of our own minds or of our patients. It is not just that the accoustics are poor, as it were, or that the actions move at too rapid and complex a pace, or that we cannot keep track of the vast array of Chekhovian characters; the trouble lies with language itself. Not only are we incapable of a perfect understanding of the meaning of any language, whether it comes from ourselves or another, but no language can capture perfectly the meaning of the inchoate thoughts it seeks to ensnare. The trouble would appear to lie in two directions: one direction is that the transformation of nascent thought into any language is rife with distortion; the other is that every language has its limit of representability. Even if we could synthesize all the symbolic forms in some super ballet-opera, we would still be left with that residue that Wittgenstein calls "what cannot be said but must be shown", the area of emotional intimacy where nothing but the contact of baby-and-breast or lovers embraced can communicate.

Treating dreams as a language is not foreign to Freud's ways of thinking at all, for he compared the analysis of dreams to the translation of a foreign language. But perhaps we would wish to take issue with him about the method involved. His own comparison of the translation of Livy from Latin to German followed the schoolboy method of first making a literal translation and then rearranging the thoughts into literate German. That may be a good enough description of "translation" but it is not the same as "reading Latin". We would wish to "read dreams": in this hope we might aspire in time to learn the dream-language of each of our many patients, but the task appears daunting if not impossible. In fact it is not the method we use, for we do not have access to the patient's dream in the same sense that we have to our own. Probably many analysts do follow a "translation" method of work, or at least they think, as Freud thought, that they do so; but experience strongly suggests that this is not what happens. In keeping with Bion's dictum of "resisting memory and desire", difficult as this may be in relation to anecdotal material or historical recollection, it comes very easily and naturally when listening to a dream. What seems to happen is that the analyst listens to the patient and watches the image that appears in his imagination. It might cogently be asserted that he allows the patient to evoke a dream in himself. Of course that is his dream and will be formed by the vicissitudes of his own personality. But after all, years of experience on the couch and of subsequent self-analysis might reasonably be expected to have given him a certain virtuosity with the language of his own dreams. From this point of view one might imagine that every attempt to formulate an interpretation of a patient's dream could imply the tacit preamble, "While listening to your dream I had a dream which in my emotional life would mean the following, which I will impart to you in the hope that it will throw some light on the meaning that your dream has for you."

You will recognize that this method does not really correspond to the "intuitionist" one which Freud abjured. Surely there are moments when intuition, even inspired intuition, enters into analytic work and evokes the "funny you should say that" type of response from the patient. And of course we intuit rather than observe the emotional atmosphere in the consulting room as it changes from moment to moment. But I would not wish to stretch the concept of intuition to say that I "intuit" French or Italian even though it might be that my imperfect knowledge of these languages and my incapacity for fluent thought or speech in their medium cannot match my comprehension when they are spoken slowly.

Perhaps the best link to earlier attitudes toward work with dreams is again Ella Sharpe's emphasis on "poetic diction" in the dream. But poetic diction is something that we all, not only Bion, consciously aspire to. We would like to be able to talk and write poetically, utilizing all the artistic devices not merely for embellishment but for richer and more precise communication of the emotional meaning that we hope lurks in our unspoken thoughts. We would hope to be able to speak to ourselves and to others in a manner that helped us to discover what we think, perhaps even what we know. And we would join with Prospero in paying respect to our dreams as the fountainhead of this knowledge of ourselves and others. But we must learn the language, to "govern the ventages", in order to have access to this "eloquent music" wherein lies the "heart of mystery" of ourselves.

But poets can be liars as well as prophets, as Plato emphasized, and we cannot look upon dreams as telling the truth, the whole truth and nothing but the truth. In so far as they tell the truth, it is the truth about how emotional experiences are dealt with in the depths of the mind, but truth is not always treasured there, for it is freighted with mental pain. Our lecturer's distance from events in Washington may be the truth about the events but it is not the truth about his distance from them. The image of the Crucifixion may be the truth about the patient's feelings about the coming termination of his analysis in terms of "Father, why hast thou forsaken me?" but it is not the truth about his capacities to struggle against the domination of his infantile greed, envy and jealousy.

Bion has given us a theory which formulates at least three methods of distorting the truth, which he has called Column 2 of the Grid, alpha-function working in reverse, and the Negative Grid. The first method, of alleging something that is known to be false to hide our ignorance of the truth, is one with which we are all familiar in clinical work and daily life. It is exemplified by our great penchant for "explaining" by adducing causal relations which we know do not exist; we say "because" when we only mean a temporal sequence of events. The second method, alpha function in reverse, can occasionally be identified in dreams, and we can see it in operation in the consulting room when patients make meaningless mincemeat of a not unreasonable interpretation. But the Negative Grid is, I suggest, still *terra incognita* which work with dreams should help us to map. In this Negative Grid we can expect to find all the devices which have been described as "mechanisms of defence", the naming of which may help us to locate them in operation but tell us little, epistemologically, about their inner workings.

Since our intention is to construct a psycho-analytical theory of dreams in the spirit of the "extended" metapsychology of Klein and Bion, we must face the complexity of the task. The epistemological aspect we have already argued, but the geographic presents some problems. Not only must we reckon with the division of the mental "world" into its various spaces, but also the lack of unity of the mind. Splitting processes divide one part from another, projective and other modes of narcissistic identification confuse the distinction between self and object while introjective identification fosters the evolution of the adult part of the personality. The distinction between the dream process and the observation of this process raises the problem which we have metaphorically described as the "theatre for the generating of meaning", and it may prove useful to follow this image in defining the varying roles of different parts of the personality *vis à vis* any particular dream as well as the geographic locality of the dream action.

In these theatrical terms, for instance, there can be little doubt that our crucified fellow is the star of the show in all four dreams while our lecturer is in the audience. We could arrange a table of organization of our theatre, a hierarchy of participation: critic, audience, producer, director, character parts, *ingénue*, male lead, female lead. Perhaps in the Brechtian spirit we could add "the Gods", descending occasionally to evaluate the progress of these mortal children.

The task would not, at the moment in our scientific history, seem quite so complex in regard to the geography, stage set, the "world" in which the drama is being enacted. These would seem to be restricted to two major possibilities: inside or outside the objects, particularly inside or outside the body of the mother. But we have already begun to learn from the study of confusional states that the world inside the mother's body may be subdivided into distinct, or at least distinguishable, sub-worlds from the point of view of their meaning.

So clearly we are going to employ Bion's "seven servants" in our investigation, remembering always that "why" means "reason" and not "cause" in the mental sphere. Why, for instance, have I omitted from my geographic list the area "nowhere" of the delusional system? I wish to exclude it from our theory because I feel, from my experience, that the delusional system is most usefully thought of as generating hallucination rather than dreaming, whether the person is awake or asleep. That is, if we take the delusional system in the sense of a "place" that is located essentially "nowhere", we imply that what goes on there has the meaning, essentially, of "nonsense", a tissue of lies, Pandemonium. It is a mental space where truth is of no interest, where no conflict between truth and lies occurs, where no reality testing, either by multiple vertices of thought, consensual validation of sensa or experimental action is relevant. The "White House" that Richard Nixon has been allowed to invade may still be the inside of the mother's breast, but once he has organized his gang it may be turned into the delusional system of "Watergate", paranoia. Once Stanley's glasses have been smashed and his drum destroyed in Pinter's *Birthday Party*, he is ready, mute and confused, to be carted off to "Monte" by Goldberg and McCann. Waking and sleeping have become an irrelevant distinction.

But to return to the personae in our Theatre for the Generating of Meaning, how are we to describe the psychological structural basis of the different roles? If we remember that we are not dismissing the distinction between consciousness as an "organ for the perception of psychic qualities", we can ask the question, "Which character in our theatre is, at the moment of dreaming, in possession of this organ?" But also, "Is it the same as the recaller and narrator of the dream during the analytical session?" We must allow for the possibility that they may not be – in fact probably usually are not – the same. This theme of distancing from the heart of the emotional conflict would appear to be the most common method of modulating mental pain, or perhaps it would be more correct to say, in order to distinguish "distancing" from "mechanism of defence", the most common way of modulating contact with the mental pain. The degree of distancing in this sense would allow us to consider Melanie Klein's concept of "denial of psychic reality" on a graduated scale, in keeping with our experience in the consulting room of the gradual approach that patients often make to their pain. It would also add a certain precision and substance to Freud's concept of "working through" which would go beyond the type of process of relinquishment which he spelled out so remarkably in *Mourning and Melancholia*.

Perhaps it has already become apparent that the model of dream-life we are constructing is at great variance with the archaeological model of the mind which is so explicit in Freud's work but still implicit in Klein's. What we have to put in its place? One answer would certainly be, "vertices", different points of view. Our model theatre with its array of participants implies a unity of drama but allows for a great diversity of viewpoint about the drama, as in the great Japanese film *Rachomon*. One can imagine taking a group of children to the theatre and asking them afterwards what the play was all about. One little girl would tell about the pretty woman with the beautiful dress, while a little boy would relate the shooting of the villain by the hero. This unity of drama and diversity of viewpoint also provides us with a vantage-point from which we can observe the basic unity of theme in serial dreams whose outward trappings seem so diverse – what I will call "dream continuity". This type of unity of drama can be both distinguished from and superimposed upon the grammatical type of unity that has already been imputed to the dreams of both our country-walker and lecturer. But dreams that may be brought to a single session do not always come from the same night; and indeed we would wish to have the means of showing the "narrative continuity" of dreams that can be spread over months and years of the psycho-analytical process.

This long process of analysis which Bion has called a "protracted dream" and which he has illustrated in *A Memoir of the Future,* is not only of interest to us in itself. We also are concerned with the relationship of these internal dramas to the actions, interests, values, plans and hopes which follow on from the dreaming process. These of course do not come under the heading of "day residue", the intake from waking life that impinges on the dream-life. What shall we call them? We are already aware from analytical work, of the relation of acting out to dreaming; or is it particularly the relation of acting out to the remembering of dreams? But beyond this spill-out of infantile drama, what of the fruitful harvest of those dreams which do succeed in grasping the nettle of mental pain, resolving a conflict, relinquishing an untenable position? We will surely wish our hypothesis about dream-life to shed some light on this question of growth and development of character. We have adopted an unequivocal position in regard to this matter, for, after all, in describing dream-life as the "theatre for the generating of meaning", we do clearly imply that the outside world is devoid of meaning until it has been generated and deployed outwards. Studies of autistic children, children with primary object failures, two-dimensionality and adhesive identifications, have given a theoretical and clinical firmness to the objectionable idea that "meaninglessness" can be a significant phenomenon in the lives of human beings.

We cannot contentedly leave this outline of the theory of dream-life without some comment on the momentous importance that certain dreams have in people's lives. Schreber's dream of being a woman in intercourse, the Wolf-man's dream of the wolves in the tree, may illustrate perfectly those haunting dreams which form the nucleus of severe psycho-pathological developments. But there are dreams, as Emily Brontë said, "which go through one's life like wine through water", enriching one's vision of the world with an intoxication of emotional colouring as never before. Or is it a heady vision that once was apprehended and lost, awaiting a dream to reinstate its dominion in the aesthetic relation to the world? When such a dream has visited our sleeping soul, how can we ever again doubt that dreams are "events" in our lives? In this dream world there is determined the great option between an optimistic and a pessimistic view, not only of our own lives, but of Life.

VII

The Interaction of Visual and Verbal
Language in Dreams*

It is difficult, in a book of this sort, to make headway with the problems to which we must now address ourselves, without attempting far more than we can hope to accomplish. We have already hurled ourselves at the mysterious problem of symbol formation in the visual area with, I think, some yield. We must now do the same in the verbal area. This takes us immediately into a confrontation with modern linguistics, semantics and psycho-linguistics, for it is necessary once again, as in the chapter on mutism in *Explorations in Autism*, to dissociate psycho-analytic thought about language from two main currents. The first of these is the current which allies itself to information theory and engineering, decoding and mathematics. The other is a more anthropological, mystical one concerned with ethical problems surrounding man's view of his own prehistory.

It may seem unnecessary to enter into this debate, but it may eventually appear that the specific dissociation from them also highlights the problem of identification in language and the deeply emotional roots of grammar. In the chapter on mutism I suggested a two-tiered structure of language, one operating from the depths of the unconscious for the purpose of transmitting states of mind through the operation of projective identification, while the other, more conscious, superimposes words upon this deep music for the purpose of communicating information about the outside world. Ecological studies suggest that both of these operate in animals, mainly the former in mammals and the latter in insects. Man has fused the two and even, in his religious history, attempted to find words for states of mind. This theological prelude to literature may have blossomed but it is clear that only a very few gifted individuals have ever mastered its subtle techniques.

In this chapter I shall try to demonstrate the foundation in dreams of this elusive art. In the clinical material I hope to be able to demonstrate something of the weaving together of the music,

*Previously published in *Language and Cognition: Essays in Honor of Arthur J. Bronstein* (Ed – Raphael) (New York, Plenum, 1983).

the verbal meanings and their evoked visual images which, placed in a kind of fugue with the manifest visual aspects of the dream, produce what Ella Sharpe has called the "poetic diction" of the dream. But first I think it is necessary to argue the case for a psycho-analytical view of linguistics. The problems of linguistics, or psycho-linguistics, which concern us are of two sorts, at two ends of a methodological spectrum. At one end is the mind-body problem dogging the footsteps of behaviourist psychologists like Skinner and mathematical linguists like Chomsky and Katz. At the other end is the problem of cosmic mysticism whose expression, in the spirit of Jung or Ouspensky, is the Whorf-Sapir theory of the relativity of language. I will discuss these in order to define the position I think psycho-analysis achieves in its methodology, and also to stress those mysterious aspects of grammar and semantics which link with our main interest, dreams.

After this linguistic preamble, I shall turn to the problem of dream structure, its relation to waking thought and to inner and outer speech, using some clinical material from a young poet, and a gifted psychotic girl.

All linguistics start with the assumption that spoken language is composed of basic units which are arranged inside the head and emitted by the oral apparatus. This is common sense and self-evident, but I will argue that it is not correct from the psycho-analytical point of view. The great cleavage in the linguistic field is over the issue of whether the primary unit of language is the phoneme (the unit of sound) or the morpheme (the unit of meaning). Those who oppose the phoneme as an artificial unit created by phonologists, on whatever ground they base their argument – psychological, methodological or theoretical – seem nonetheless to assume that a "unit" must be found.

The reason for this is apparent, for all linguists seem to assume that language has the primary function of communicating information. For example, to quote from Roman Jakobson and Morris Halle: "The addressee of a coded message is supposed to be in possession of the code and through it he interprets the message. Unlike the decoder, the cryptanalyst comes into possession of a message with no prior knowledge of the underlying code and must break this code through dextrous manipulation of the message. A native speaker responds to any text in his language as a regular decoder, whereas a stranger, unfamiliar with the language, faces the same text as a cryptanalyst. A linguist, approaching a totally unknown language, starts as a cryptanalyst until, through a gradual breaking of the code, he finally succeeds in approaching any message in this language like a native decoder."

It is apparent that this is not a model, simile or metaphor, but a statement. It places speaker and listener in relation to one another as tuned instruments. This is the basic hypothesis of Noam Chomsky's work as well, and seems to pay no heed whatsoever to the meaning of speaker-listener as two instances in the life history of two organisms. In fact, none of the writers who takes this mechanistic approach in methodology believes in its reality. Jakobson and Halle write: "The code of features used by the listener does not exhaust the information he receives from the sounds of the incoming message. From its sound shape he extracts clues to the identity of the sender."

We need only examine the information content of the "identity of the sender" to recognize that it is fantastic, something like the ratio of dot-dash in telegraphy to the number of dots at any moment on a TV screen. But a dog can look at a TV screen and see nothing, as a savage or a child can look into a mirror and at first see nothing. Evidently the idea of a code derives from the problem of transmitting verbal messages by non-verbal means. One may say that Michael Ventris and John Chadwick decoded Linear B by a "dexterous manipulation of the message" but only as a result of a fair knowledge of both the language and the culture involved.

Another source of confusion of mind and brain in linguistic theory, in addition to this great reliance on communication, derives from neurology and neurophysiology. The study of aphasia, to which Freud made a classical contribution before ever he developed the psycho-analytical method, is a rich source of ideas about language function. But also a source of serious pitfalls. First of all, despite the capacity of able observers to classify aphasias, every case is different to a significant degree, the more so when the damage is cortical rather than in deeper, pathway structures. The patterns of aphasic difficulties stand in relation to the language symptoms of mental illness as those of organic paralyses or anaesthesias do in relation to hysterical ones. We can distinguish by pattern in a manner that is comparable to the way in which the aeronautical "black box" technique distinguishes between the pattern of a machine failure and an error in human judgment in an air crash. The loss of language in regressive mental illness such as catatonic schizophrenia has no resemblance in pattern to an aphasia, nor does the mutism of the autistic child resemble the "pattern" of mutism in the mental defective.

This differentiation between man and machine, between mind and brain, is essential for further discussion. Clearly machines do not — and never will — "talk", any more than planes will "fly". Birds fly, they live on the air; machines can only propel themselves through the air from place to place. The thing that amuses us so much when we see a swan run splashing and flapping across the water is that his ungainliness is like an aeroplane, although we forget this clumsiness when we watch a jet liner make its run.

Humans live linguistically. It is essential to their humanity. "Speech is the best show man puts on", Benjamin Lee Whorf writes. Probably Susanne Langer's grasp of the peculiar concatenation of social impulses, lalling impulse and symbolization impulse which drives the child to become "speaking", comes closer to the psycho-analytical theory. But, as we shall see, the key concept, identification, is still missing. Surely the most brilliant work in linguistics struggling to cross from brain to mind as its central preoccupation is that of Noam Chomsky. With a rich philological, semantic and phonological background, and under the influence of communication engineering, he has set out to utilize the philosophical direction set by Russell, Wittgenstein and Carnap to investigate syntax by divorcing its formal qualities from the semantic aspects. He does this by constructing a "generative grammar" composed of the rules of transformation of strings of morphemes. The impossible aim is to invent a universal grammar that would differentiate the grammatical from the agrammatical in any language regardless of whether the sentence in question was meaningful, meaningless or even unthinkable. Of course he is faced with the task of closing the gap exposed by intuition in the initial stages of his theorizing, for he acknowledges that the division grammatical–agrammatical is in the first instance an intuitive judgment. He also acknowledges that a distinction between surface and depth must be made in grammar, as in meaning, as described by Wittgenstein. But nonetheless he pushes on to insist that in learning language a child must invent a grammar before he can comprehend what is being said. We know that a child, like Koehler's apes, could hardly "invent" a simple tool such as joining two sticks together to reach the bananas without being "taught". The question, from Augustine to Wittgenstein, has been the nature of "teaching".

In what follows, the concept of "intuition" will be given finer definition and the concept of "learning" will be firmly linked to that of "teaching" to define the context in which speech develops in the child. But first we must consider the other side of the spectrum in linguistic theory where "intuition" is not eschewed, but embraced as a cosmic mysticism which needs to be distinguished from the mystical element in psycho-analysis.

There is an evasion of the problem of the individual mind and its extraordinary development from birth onward which is common to religion in the past and anthropology in the present. Jerrold Katz calls it a "theological" type of "mentalism" in dissociating his own work and that of Chomsky from the suspicion of dealing with "mind" as synonymous with "soul" or "spirit". Clearly their conception of mind is far too neurophysiological for any such link and can hardly be dissociated from the mindlessness of behaviourism which knows nothing of mind but only of the "summation of behaviour". But psycho-analysis has a very distinct link with theology, both in its essentially introspective method and its findings. While all theologies find godhead external to the individual, psycho-analysis finds it internal, and here differs from the psychology of Jung or the mysticism of Ouspensky. The form which this cosmic mysticism takes in linguistic science comes from the anthropologists and is exemplified in the work of Korzybski. The central idea is that the culture, through its language, imposes limitations on the modes of thought of the individual, thereby attributing to language and culture a reality and continuity which is primary rather than secondary in respect to the individual. In a sense it places culture in relation to the individual as Mendelian; Darwinian theory places the species in relation to the individual member.

But everything indicates that heredity in the realm of the mind is thoroughly Lamarckian – that is, derived from the acquired characteristics in transmission from generation to generation both in form and content, or, in the case of language, both in syntax and semantics. A certain anti-civilization spirit intrudes upon that type of anthropology which sees a superior virtue in the primitive which o'erleaps itself in opposing what it thinks is the prevalent attitude of contempt. But it is wrong to think that scientific workers in the field consider "primitive" or even "aboriginal" groups as inferior in intelligence, any more than one thinks of the child in this respect. Whorf admires the Hopi Indian's model of the universe and considers his tense-less language quite satisfactory because of his unification of space-time: "The Hopi language is capable of accounting for and describing correctly, in a pragmatic or operational sense, all observable phenomena of the universe. Hence, I find it gratuitous to assume that Hopi thinking contains any such notions as the supposed intuitively felt flowing of "time", or that the intuition of a Hopi gives him this as one of its data. Just as it is possible to have any number of geometries other than the Euclidean which give an equally perfect account of space configuration, so it is possible to have descriptions of the universe, all equally valid, that do not contain our familiar contrasts of time and space. The relativity viewpoint of modern physics is one such view, conceived in mathematical terms, and the Hopi Weltanschauung is another and quite different one, non-mathematical and linguistic."

Of course, the whole problem resides in the idea of "capable of accounting for and describing". It is a kind of anthropophilia which wishes to see special virtue in the primitive, and generously projects into the savage mind, much as people project into children, that peculiar and incompatible mixture of innocence and creativity by which their idealization is consummated. It stems from a distrust of the concepts of development, of individuality and of the adult-infantile differentiation as a qualitative one. We will come later to this point of distinguishing between child and grown-up as a descriptive antithesis, and infantile-adult as a metapsychological one.

The mystical element, on the other hand, in psycho-analytical theory resides not in its modes of thought but in the "facts" of mental life which it appears to discover. It takes the concept "creative" to mean more than what Chomsky means when he writes: "In fact, a real understanding of how a language can (in Humboldt's words) 'make infinite use of finite means', has developed only within the last thirty years, in the course of studies in the foundations of mathematics. Now that these concepts were readily available it was possible to return to the problems that were raised, but not solved, in traditional linguistic theory: and to attempt an explicit formulation of the 'creative' processes of language. By 'creative', psychoanalysts mean something more like 'raise to a new level of self-perpetuating orderliness'".

The nature of the cosmic mysticism contained in such a theory of the relativity of language may not seem one that impinges as a serious problem on one's thinking, until its implication for epistemological theory is recognized. The theory of knowledge implied in Ouspensky's book gives concreteness to words as containing meaning in themselves, as full and therefore available for exploration. It indicates that all knowledge *exists* and *awaits* discovery. The mind of God manifests itself in the word.

Psycho-analysis also has a mystical element which relates to epistemology, but it places the scene of transactions differently and sees the relation to language in a more creative sense. Thus we may recognize the primal combined object, breast and nipple, as truly the source of knowledge, since thinking is an unconscious mental activity whose scene is the baby-breast relationship; that is, internal *teaching* means that the breast knows everything, in a categorical sense. It is omniscient, contains all knowledge – not of course in terms of external reality but as a category of meaning in psychic reality. The words, given as empty containers by external objects, are filled with meaning by the internal breast. But this is a life-time process, by which experiences may be assimilated to fill with meaning the verbal categories in ever expanding levels of abstraction. The filling of old words with new meaning need never

101

destroy or even overwhelm or obscure their old meaning, so mar-
vellously contextual in actual language usage is the selection of the
particular aspect of a word's multitudinous contents. More suspect
as a process is the invention of new words – or at least new morphemes. The taxonomic aspect of scientific investigation has always avoided this problem by the appropriation of Greek and
Latin morphemes for compounding into names for objects or processes of enquiry. In a pre-scientific era in any field, before "facts"
have been delineated, a phenomenon described by someone tends
to have his name stuck to it as an identification tag, like Spoonerism
or Bright's disease. These are not really new morphemes but,
rather like the mathematician's x and y, identification tags for un-
knowns.

One would expect, therefore, that the lexical evolution of language would involve an *apparent* continual expansion and a *real*
continual simplification at the morpheme level. In this way the
language of science describing the outer world, and the language
of poetry describing the inner world, can be seen to follow the
same basis of development. Psycho-analysis bridges this gap for
the first time in the unique direction, a scientific poetry. Poetic
science, on the other hand, is as old as religion.

Having examined some of the work in modern linguistic theory
and its relation to psycho-analysis in both methodology and basic
premises, we may move on to examine the relation of language to
image as seen in the analysis of dreams. A psycho-analytical conception of language function should enable us to examine and
formulate the problem of the interaction of words and images in
dreams.

I shall present clinical material from two patients to illustrate
two different aspects of the problem. First, material of a gifted
poet will be used to show how deep are the roots of language in
unconscious plastic phantasy. Second, material of a chronic
psychotic painter will be brought to show the fundamentally non-
verbal nature of vocalization and its relation to infantile babblings.

A young poet, under the influence of recent high praise of his
latest volume, shortly after the Christmas break and approaching
the week-end, brought this dream. *He was going to the home of
Elizabeth Taylor and Richard Burton to borrow a car, which, in the dream,
was in fact the car he owns. It seemed necessary to go from the gravelled
drive, through the house into the garden to reach the rear where the car was
parked. There was a huge party going on, in house and garden, and, since
he had not beeen invited, he pushed his way through the crowd averting his
gaze so as not to be stopped in conversation by people he knew, lest he be
thought by the Burtons to be gate-crashing. In the garden a commotion was
going on around a little pavilion which was a First Aid Station; a young*

woman named Miss Spoonerism had died and was being carried out on a stretcher. When a woman called to him, he greeted her as "Elizabeth" but she said she was not Elizabeth and he realized that it was the secretary or someone whom he seemed to know. He told her a lie – that he had come to return Elizabeth's car, and pressed on.

His assocaiations were that he and his wife were invited to lunch that day by the ex-wife, also named Elizabeth, of a movie star, also named Richard. But he decided not to go. He could not remember exactly what a Spoonerism was and had looked it up, as he had once before, and found the example "crushing blow – blushing crow". In the dream there was nothing strange in the name Miss Spoonerism, no joke or unreality.

The essential elements I wish to emphasize are: the passage through from front to rear, the intrusion, the mis-identification, the lying reversal, the death, the associated equivocation regarding the marital status of the two Elizabeth-Richard couples, and the equivocation about his welcome (avoiding greetings yet fearful of being accused of gate-crashing.)

The analytic background of the dream is very important. This patient had lost his father at an early age and his mother had never remarried, though much sought after by men and passionate in her nature. The patient was married to a charming girlish woman who was experienced by him, as documented by innumerable dreams, as a part of his mother, namely the breast-buttock with which he had an erotic and possessive relationship. Since he allowed no father in his inner world but presided there himself as the little husband, the differentiation of levels adult-infantile was extremely confused. He could not, therefore, in his infantile omnipotence recognize that he treated his women badly from a manly point of view. This was repeated in the maternal transference in the analysis, in which his love affair with the analytic method produced the feeling of being the ideal patient, so that he could never recognize how he controlled his material, denigrated the analyst as the father, and begrudged respect and gratitude to both father and mother aspects of the analyst – represented specifically in insisting that he could only pay a low fee as his future income was uncertain.

The prolonged struggle over these issues had been broken momentarily just before the holiday when he had volunteered to pay the regular fee under the pressure of depressive anxiety about the analyst's safety, stirred by a very disturbing dream in which *his mother, hand to her breast, complained of his selfishness, that after a heavy meal he just goes off to a party with his wife, leaving her to worry about their baby.* But the differentiation and insight was lost almost immediately after the holiday break and the old struggle resumed.

Thus the dream came under the pressure of having received a bill which he was neglecting to pay without reason, and even neglecting to mention.

During the session of the "Miss Spoonerism" dream the patient was resistant to the analysis but came to the next session in a different mood, paid his bill and brought material which had been withheld. What he had neglected to reveal in the previous session was that he was planning that night to see a new film starring the Burtons, in which Elizabeth played the part of a dying woman with no husband.

The analysis of the dream was, in substance, as follows: in it we saw once again the intrusive little boy (the gate-crasher) who would not allow Mummy (Elizabeth) to be married to Daddy (Richard – the divorced one whose wife's invitation to lunch he planned to refuse) because he could not resist borrowing and owning the breast (his white car) which he thought he reached by going inside the mother's genital in intercourse (the party), since he was so confused between breast and buttock (front drive and back garden). In this confusion he could not comprehend the idea of being unwelcome to Mummy's genital when he was invited to her breast (luncheon invitation by the other Elizabeth), but avoided noticing the signs of being unwelcome (averting his gaze as he pushed through the crowd) and lied about his intentions (to return rather than to borrow the car.) Only when we link the dream to that before the holiday (his mother with hand-to-breast complaining of his selfishness) and the film he was planning to see the following evening (of the dying divorcée), can we understand that the seemingly irrelevant death of Miss Spoonerism means that the Mummy who treats the little boy's intrusiveness and his confusing front (breast and genital) with back (buttock and rectum) as a joke (blushing crow), is a dying Mummy (crushing blow) due to lack of love (the dying divorcée, visited in the film only by a gigolo, the Angel of Death). The dream of a poet, gifted to a high degree, in both visual and verbal representation.

In the case of our dreamer, we have already formulated his material in so far as it refers to the structure of the transference and his internal situation with its genital references. Let us now turn to its linguistic reference. Our poet's reliance upon language as an omnipotent tool can be traced to a very early time in his life. It was a matter of family folklore how, at the age of six, he had routed with a stream of logic and invective some political police of his native country who had come to investigate in his father's absence. He was also proud of the speed and totality with which he had changed from his native tongue to English in his pre-pubertal years. His verbal gifts took him into the world at an early age, cutting short his formal education. His facility with language enabled him to converse freely with educated persons in a wide variety of fields to a degree which hid, not only from others but from himself, the shallowness of his understanding of science, history, philosophy, mathematics, economics, politics, etc. His wit was equally reliable as a weapon against persecutors and as a tool of seduction.

Similarly his contact with unconscious phantasy was unusually detailed and consistent. Seldom did he come to a session without a dream, vividly recalled and ably communicated in both its visual and affective content.

The linguistic elements manifest in the dream are as follows:—

1. equation of objects through equation of their names — the two Elizabeth–Richard couples. By this equation he was able to uncouple them at the verbal level.
2. the many levels at which the reversal of meaning is worked over in the dream and associations – going from the front garden to the rear garage; the reversal of borrow–return; the balance of Elizabeth–not–Elizabeth; the uncertainty of guest–gate-crasher; the contrast of party–death.
3. this contrast of party–death also highlights the manner in which affects are reversed and is the key to the defensive use of the Spoonerism as a form of humour, as in crushing blow–blushing crow. Thus we are dealing with a manic defence against depressive pain, the items of which can be listed from the dream as follows:

   the divorcing of the Elizabeth–Richard couple;
   the gate-crashing;
   the borrowing of the car, presumably without permission.

All these acts of selfishness, which cause the mother to put her hand to her breast and threaten the crushing blow of her death, are reversed by the Spoonerism joke and his manic reparative lie that he is returning the car. The death of Miss Spoonerism therefore means that he must choose between the death of his mother, and the death of his unmarried wife–breast, Miss S., who thinks little boys' verbal tricks are so funny that their intrusiveness should be forgiven. It is of interest to note that the meaning of the breast is altered, by the death of Miss Spoonerism, from the white car he came to borrow to the First Aid Pavilion, thereby also differentiating breast from buttock (the white car in the back of the genital house–garden party).

The syntactic implications are of special interest. Coming, as the dream does, at a point in the analysis when insight has begun to alter the economic balance between paranoid-schizoid and depressive (Ps ‹—› D) relations to internal objects and in the transference, it can be seen to have a structure which I have come to call the "T-junction" structure because of its most unequivocal type of representation in dreams. Its phrase structure can be seen as: "I used to..., but since..., I now...". Namely: "I used to feel free to intrude into Mummy's and Daddy's sexual relationship, borrowing Mummy's bottom for my pleasure, concerned only that other people should not think that I did so without Mummy's permission, but since the death of her sense of humour about my selfishness, I now realize that it is a lie when I say that by defecating I return something borrowed from her, and anyhow I realize that such intimacies have only been allowed by the maid and not by Mummy at all."

The thesis that understanding and speaking "language" comes to children before the use of "words" implies that language is a deeply unconscious process and not, as Freud was inclined to think, one which takes place between conscious and pre-conscious levels (topographically speaking) as a means of anchoring thought in consciousness. In distinguishing between the use of language and the use of words, we imply that it is this transition which has a certain topographic significance, not the presumed process of changing image to language.

Another way of stating the same idea would be to distinguish between the use of language as a mode of operation of projective identification – that is, for the communication of states of mind – while words are used for the transmission of information from mind to mind. The former involves a degree of regression to narcissism in that object–self boundaries are in some measure surrendered or obscured for the moment.

This does not, however, correspond to Piaget's "egocentric speech" of children, which is really vocalized inner speech. It may be useful, for instance, to distinguish between two types of unintelligibility. This egocentric speech, in its early stages, corresponds to infantile "babbling", in which the child expects to be as well understood by its external object as it apparently is by its internal one. In contrast are those mistakes based on homonymity, inaccurate reproduction of morphemes, reversals of phonemes of the Spoonerism type, substitution of antonyms, unconscious *double-entrendres*, dangling particles and so on. These comprise children's "howlers" which so entertain the adult world. In the "Miss Spoonerism" dream I have illustrated the way in which unconscious plastic phantasy and the verbal manipulation are linked. In that instance the material came from a highly gifted and not-very-ill adult. When we turn to very psychotic patients, we find evidence of the first type of difficulty – of babbling language – in which again a certain confusion, but this time of phonemes and of underlying thought, is in evidence. It also produces a "drunk" type of humour often employed by comics.

For example, a woman in her mid-thirties, but still looking a frail, pretty, pubertal child, had been in hospital for eight years variously considered manic-depressive or catatonic at different times. Her life on the ward was divided between lifeless periods in bed and driven activity as a scullery maid and general dogsbody under the tyrannical control of another chronic patient, Millie, who had something of a coterie. With this clique Millie seemed to my patient to dominate the ward and intimidate the staff. The peace was only occasionally broken by someone – my patient included – "going up the wall" or "smashing". The former consisted of screaming assertiveness, and the latter of breaking dishes and crockery. These outbreaks were attributed to various intrusions from staff or visitors into Millie's Pax Romana, "If only they would let us alone", she often said. The analysis, to which the patient was being brought by car and nurse, was limited by her to two sessions per week as the maximum intrusion into this status quo that she could tolerate.

As the Easter break in analysis approached she began "smashing", "going up the wall", and attempting suicide on returning to the hospital after each session. But she struggled against these states, had herself put in a seclusion room and cooperated very well in the sessions. To the penultimate session she brought the following dreams:

1. *Millie was cutting and handing about lettuce*
2. *Amy might smash a little tank outside her room.*

Associations, sometimes stimulated by the analyst's enquiring noises or repetition of words from the dream, brought further information. Sometimes they have lettuce with the meals, but there was no meal with the dream. Amy is a "smasher" and gets upset at holidays when the ward empties of its less permanent residents as relatives take the less ill home for visiting. The "tank" was of glass, big enough to hold about a pint, with graduations like a thermometer. The dreams were interpreted as meaning: if you would let us alone (lettuce alone) and not stir the feelings of love (Amy), we would not destroy our capacity (holding about a pint) for gratitude (t(h)ank) when left alone (Easter break).

It is characteristic of the patient as she totters from the room at the end of the session to mumble tearfully at the door, either "msoy" (I'm sorry) if she has brought no dreams, or "thany" (thank you) if she has. She weeps on the trip back to the hospital and is filled by suicidal impulses to throw herself from the car, strangle herself with her scarf, poison herself with secreted pills.

One can see clearly the image, as of concentration camp children, huddled together in utter aversion to the brutality of the adult world, scavenging for food and sharing it out, their slogan "let us alone", "lettuce alone" and "ledusalown" in ever louder, more defiant, more dysarthric chant, "LESALON".

Outside the door of the consulting room is the mad-house of the adult world where she had drifted in confusion from bed to bed during the years before hospitalization, searching for a love-object, that is, an object to fill her with love. But it would have to be an interminable and uninterrupted process, for the removal of the nipple from her mouth (the tank—baby bottle outside Amy's door) confronts her with the fact of having emptied her object. This fact renders her gratitude so painful that she smashes the object and thus her perception of the sacrifice it made for her, her capacity to remember the feed, her realization of a good object. "Let us alone". "Say thank you". "Lettuce alone". "Say thanks". LESALON!!! TANK!!

By extrapolating the phonemic implication of the two dreams within the social situation to which they refer, namely the ward of the mental hospital on the one hand, and the analytic situation on the other, I have hoped to demonstrate the language deterioration which is a marked trend in this patient. Not only does the morphemic structure seem to melt away into confused homonymity, but the concreteness of the image ("lettuce alone" and "tank") seems to enter into an oscillating, echoing relation to the phonemic structure. The extrapolation to drunken babbling is, I think, an unmistakable trend. The main point is that the "language" is nonetheless preserved, despite the flux of morphemic, phonemic and syntactic structures. In the two images, Millie passing out the lettuce and Amy with the tank outside her door, the language of "let us alone" and "thank you" is preserved in the childish sense in which inner speech develops, in ignorance of words and grammar, as statements of states of mind, namely *withdrawal* and *indebtedness* respectively.

I suggest that language is primarily a function of unconscious phantasy which employs projective identification as its mode of communication. The substance of its communications are states-of-mind. Its means of communication are fundamentally primitive, namely song and dance. As its motive is the communication of states-of-mind, its information content relates primarily to psychic reality, and thus to the realm of experience relevant to art, religion, courting and combat. The subtlety of its content as regards range and intensity of emotion, complexity, levels of abstraction and logical operations, is such as can only be approximated verbally by the poet. Its history must, of course, have antedated verbal language by innumerable millenia and have reached the present level of development at a time in prehistory when communication of information about external reality was still limited to pointing. This same sequence is repeated in childhood development where the elaborate communication between mother and child, consisting of sound and gesture approximating to song and dance, stands in marked contrast to the difficulty of pointing-and-naming in regard to the facts of external reality.

We are thus suggesting a two-step theory of language development: a first step consisting of the realization by the child of its instinctual capacity for inner language, for the internal and external "public-ation" (Bion) of states-of-mind; and a second step consisting of the adaptation of this language to the description of external reality by means of verbalization, meaning the delineation of morphemes within the "strings" (Chomsky) of phonemes. In this conception, grammar or syntax is seen as a function of inner language. Hence its delineation is necessarily intuitive, placing the grammarian in the position of an after-the-fact judgment of the grammatic–agrammatic differentiation which has no more validity as a value judgment than to say that French is inferior to English. This I believe is the point that Whorf would like to make but, lacking the conceptual equipment to distinguish between internal and external language, miscarries into irrelevantly pleading the moral equality of primitive language. Chomsky, on the other hand, being bound to an information-theory conception of language, conceives of a grammar as conventional, a carrier for bits of meaning which can be introduced into the empty containers of the carrier in infinite variation, some sensical and others non-sensical.

In our theory, grammar would stand in an absolutely bound relation to the language of unconscious phantasy in something of the same relation as a scale of tones stands to a body of music; or as the particular set of axioms stands in relation to the body of a particular geometry; or as a particular set of "natural rights" stands in relation to a body of law and what the courts will do in fact.

In this sense Chomsky is right to think that grammar "generates" language, but not because of the existence of a set of "rules" separate from meaning. Rather it is a set of basic meanings in relation to time, space, person and logical operations which determine the transformation of inner language into inner speech through verbalization. In a sense Freud was right to think that words had a special relation to consciousness, since attention, which is the special province of consciousness, is directed by verbalization towards items of perception which otherwise would not command it, just as movement of an item in a static visual field immediately commands attention.

Ernst Cassirer has treated language as one of the many possible symbolic forms by which cognition may objectify itself through and in the action of the mind. In this way he has applied Kant's principles of form in epistemology so as to get beyond the usual philosophical bias of considering the word and the idea to be identical. I say "bias", for philosophers are "verbal" people, as artists are "visual" and musicians "auditory" in their spontaneous preferred mode of representation. It is a view to which I believe Chomsky also came later. It is a view which is implicit in the psycho-analytical theory of the mind, even though Freud himself equivocated to some extent. At least one cannot really tell how his earlier topographic view of the stratification of the mind in terms of levels of consciousness and his later structural concept fuse with one another in regard to the relationship of verbalization to thought. There is very little to be found outside the "Project" (1897) and Ch. VII of the *Interpretation of Dreams* (1900), which are both, in a sense, pre-analytic from the point of view of clinical method of enquiry. My impression is that word and symbol remained very closely bound in his mind as representations of meaning in a far more rigid sense than Wittgenstein's "seeing as", and in a far more restricted sense in regard to the meaning of words than Russell's meta-levels. The concept of perception as a creative–active process did not really enter psycho-analytical thought until the work of Paul Schilder. Freud's concept of perceptual consciousness was, for instance, a far more photographic, "copy" theory.

How far have we come in our argument? In effect I have brought some clinical material, especially the dreams of a neurotic poet and a psychotic painter, to broach the thesis that language in its truest meaning is a process that emerges from unconscious phantasy; that formal representations of various sorts organize these phantasies in the publishable forms which can serve as modes of communication of mental states. Language is one of these several forms. Any formed representation may be built secondarily into a notational system for communicating information about external reality. This adaptation is accomplished by a kind of ellipsis which omits mention of the cognitive process, as for instance in Russell's "I am cat-perceptive" as the correct semantic form for "It is a cat". A tertiary system may represent this in turn, as in written language or musical notation.

The question now arises as to whether words are a system of notation by means of which people exchange information about language as a phenomenon or object of cognition in the outside world; or do they, in themselves, comprise a symbolic form, by means of which cognition is represented in the mind? Language we accept as a symbolic form. But words? Morphemes? Phonemes? Letters? Ideograms? Hieroglyphics? I suggest that we consider "vocalization" as the symbolic form and "verbalization" as its corresponding notational system.

But where does this leave us in regard to grammar? If we return to our two dreamers, we may most cogently express the answer to this question in terms of the linguistic analyses of the two sets of dreams. In the case of our poet, the theme of the dream overall is that something formerly amused mother and no longer does, and that furthermore the patient himself has begun to understand that it is not funny in the sense of witty–amusing but only in the sense of triumphant–amusing. The joke at the level of language of unconscious phantasy involves a little boy who is such an amusing little gate-crasher at Mummy's bottom that she does not really need any other sexual partner. But Mummy-with-her-hand-to-her-breast has put a stop to this joke. The symbolic form at this level is visual phantasy.

But the dream hints that the same joke has a representation in another symbolic form, vocalization, called technically "Spoonerism". Associations of the patient indicate this to be the juxtaposition of crushing-blow: blushing crow. One would be inclined to think that jokes of this sort were the dysarthric "drunken" type of humour so popular with children and leave the matter there, as if it were explained. It would be as if to say that the custard-pie-in-the-face "just is" funny.

Freud's approach to wit goes some distance to account for the emotionality tapped by jokes, but does very little to explain why the joke is funny, or to investigate different categories of humour. Again this work was pre-analytic from the methodological point of view. Nothing but the method of clinical psycho-analysis could plumb the depths of the humour in a Spoonerism and demonstrate its immediate source of comic effect in the pre-verbal roguishness of a little boy.

In other words I am suggesting that in the case of the particular Spoonerism, the humour comes from below the level of verbalization, and has, fundamentally, nothing to do with words or the speaker's mistake but with meaning and its reversal. In its vocalized form the humour had adopted a verbal context for its expression. Had the dream of our psychotic painter been instead a charade acted out as a game at a party, the humour would have been, presumably, a pun on the homonymous words "Let us alone" and "lettuce alone". It was not a joke, but rather demonstrated that the patient's regression in her dreams and in the transference has proceeded to a pre-verbal type of vocalization, characteristic of pre-school childhood, in which homonymity of sound is taken as identity of meaning. We might conclude then that the hypothetical charade at the party would involve a bit of humour whose unconscious determination involved some juxtaposition of adult and infantile mentality in which confusion at infantile level was held up to ridicule cruelly as older children may with younger ones, or gently appreciated as adults may with young children.

We seem, therefore, to have elaborated a two-tier theory of speech; that it consists of a system of vocalization as the publishable symbolic form of one current of unconscious phantasy, and therefore of thought; and that this vocalization lends itself as verbalization to a notational system for the communication of information about the outside world. Accordingly we think that grammar is also two-tiered. Depth (unconscious) grammar includes the phonemic–morphemic elements of vocalization in all its musical aspects (including the postural and mimed aspects related to dance and dramatization) as well as the logical operations of syntax which are implied in the juxtapositions contained in the unconscious phantasy sequence. Surface grammar contains all those modifications of vocalization which the communication of information about the external world requires in order to minimize the many possible forms of ambiguity – and therefore confusion.

Colloquial speech is poorly equipped for this latter task and is notoriously "agrammatical" in the sense of surface grammar. But correspondingly, speech which is grammatically correct in this surface sense is notoriously poor for the communication of states of mind. Dare we suggest that the *technical* skill of the poet resides exactly here, in the bringing together of depth and surface grammars?

In a peculiar way, this is precisely the view to which Noam Chomsky seems to arrive when he reviews the history of linguistic thought (from Descartes, through the "Port Royal" grammarians, to von Humboldt, Leibniz, and to modern philosophy).

What contribution, then, has this chapter attempted to make to our general theory of dreams? Its main task has been to refute Freud's finding that language in dreams has merely been lifted from the day residue and does not in any way imply thought within the dream process. But we have also tried to put in its place a concept of vocalization in dreams as a linguistic symbolic form which stands in a fugue relation to the visual image of the dream as plastic symbolic form. In preferring to relate the two as "fugue" rather than to speak of them as "parallel" we would wish to imply a creative interaction by means of which the two symbolic forms potentiate one another in capturing meaning. This brings to a new poignancy Ella Sharpe's delineation of the "poetic diction" of the dream process and builds a bridge to the field of aesthetics in general. It would seem to open up to investigation the area of "composition" of the dream as an aesthetic object. But perhaps this understanding of the structuring of dreams may also feed back to aesthetics as an aid to investigate composition in the various fields of art, a huge undertaking richly begun by Adrian Stokes in his many publications.

VIII

The Borderland between Dreams and Hallucinations

By setting dreams at the germinal point of nascent thought, Bion has evolved a theory of thinking that implies a pattern of interaction of phenomena which clinical study should either succeed in discovering or, by failing to do so, can then declare the theory to be useless (correct or incorrect not being apposite terms in this field). The central implication of the theory of alpha-function and the Grid is, I would say, this: if an emotional experience is not worked upon by alpha-function so as to evolve alpha-elements (symbols?) which can be used for the formation of dream thoughts, and thus lend itself to digestion as nourishment for the growing mind, the emotional experience must undergo some other process in order to unburden the psychic apparatus of accretions of stimuli. Some of these processes are essentially evacuatory; some simulate digestion but evolve a system of lies which are the poison of the mind and inhibit its growth; others produce a kind of encystment or encapsulating containment and occupy areas of the mental apparatus which thereby becomes unavailable for integration in the growth process. This analogy with the metabolic processes is not employed by Bion as metaphor *per se*, but rather as a description of the workings of the mental apparatus which has evolved itself, he suggests, on the basis of analogy with the metabolic system.

Let us set aside the third type of process, encystment, to be examined in another context, assuming at the moment that it corresponds to autism. It is rather with the first two, the processes of evacuation and of toxic digestion, that we are concerned, since they bear upon the general theory of dreaming and the psychopathology of the dreaming process. Bion has suggested that if the emotional experience, or, more correctly, the perception of the emotional experience, is not worked upon by alpha-function, its elements tend to remain as disparate bits of psychic stimulation which he has called beta-elements. (One would have thought that the reverse order of naming, alpha and beta, would have been more reasonable, but Bion may have had his reasons.) For instance, he may have thought that some attempt at alpha-function always takes place but can at times become impeded, change into reverse gear as it were, and cannibalize the evolving alpha-elements, producing what he called "beta-elements with traces of ego and superego". (See the final chapter of Book III of *The Kleinian Development*).

In his earliest elucidation of this theory, Bion had suggested that the products of alpha-function formed a kind of continuous membrane of nascent thought which functioned as a "contact barrier" to differentiate conscious from unconscious. I would suggest that it would be more useful to say "between internal and external" lest it be thought that we are returning to the old topographic idea of unconscious as opposed to the systematic use of the term. In its systematic use by Freud, which later developed into the Structural Theory, system ucs. corresponds in all respects to "internal world" in the Kleinian sense of geography of mental spaces, so long as the term "conscious" is reserved for the products of the "organ of consciousness" whose function is "the perception of psychic qualities". The intention here is not to plead that this is a better use of the term, but rather it is stressed for the sake of keeping clear the meaning of the technical language we are using. For in the extended metapsychology which we are employing, the differentiation between internal world phenomena and external ones is a *sine qua non* of sanity, just as the differentiation between good and bad is central to mental health.

Conceptually very close to Bion's idea of the membrane of the contact barrier, are Esther Bick's ideas about the function of the skin as the primitive container of the personality. She sees its integrity and durability as a reflection of the mother's containing capacity, a prelude to the introjection of the combined object, nipple and breast, which epitomizes the internal rigid supporting structure – the move from an "invertebrate" to a "vertebrate" model of the personality, one might say. But with regard to the functions of dreaming, we are more concerned with the action of differentiation between external and internal worlds than with the theme of containment, the consequence of whose inadequacy is collapse rather than delusion. One can see that the meaning of the skin of the body, and its mental counterpart, approximate to Bion's contact barrier. Correspondingly the orifices of the body or actual (or potential) breaches in the integrity of the skin, are likely to have the meaning of portals of entry to the internal world, and thus to the system ucs. We do not ordinarily, in our anatomical literal-mindedness, think of eyes as orifices, perhaps more often of ears, since the membrane of the drum is not in sight. But without a doubt, for children – and the unconscious – eyes are prime portals, along with mouth, nose, ears, anus, vagina, urethra.

In the area of hallucination eyes and ears are the two most important foci of disturbance, although they are not necessarily the most frequently afflicted with hallucinatory experiences, or what Bion prefers to call "transformations in hallucinosis". Probably the senses of taste and smell are far more frequent sites. Properly we should also include the vast area of skin hallucinations, such as itching, tickling, burning pain, but we seldom think of these as hallucinatory until they are coupled with delusional ideas, as in delusions of formication. It is, by and large, the distance receptors that claim our attention because the hallucinatory phenomena which inhabit them give rise to anxiety connected to the clear-cut problem of location and therefore of reality, external versus internal. Psychiatry has traditionally drawn the distinction between "illusion" and "delusion", depending on the existence of an external stimulus. It has been reluctant to call a misidentification in the street or the hearing one's name called in a public situation, a delusion or hallucination, compared with the same phenomenon in an unpeopled situation. But it is not useful for our purposes to draw such a distinction. Common as such events may be in "normal" people and insignificant as they may be in regard to overall mental health, we must not remove them from our relevant phenomenology. In fact when we make a link between hallucination and dreaming, we imply that auditory and visual hallucination would naturally be the central phenomenon of study since they are the pre-eminent media for dream representation.

Accordingly we must wrestle with another unaccustomed idea in relation to these two organs, the reversibility of their functions. We may think of eyes as expressive, in the sense that they manifest and communicate states of mind, but it is not their visual function that performs these operations. We may think of piercing looks, "if looks could kill", and so forth, but we do not ordinarily, except in children's cartoons, think of daggers actually being emitted by the eyes. It is not enough to think that the same apparatus may be adapted to more than one function. Bion means this reversibility in a more precise sense: eyes that can take in images can also emit, project, images. And so may ears, tongues, finger tips, noses and the body orifices. Nor does he mean merely a confusion of function, as an anus may be confused with a vagina. The emotive impact of a spitting mouth is not to be accounted for simply on the basis of confusion.

Our comprehension of Bion's vision of reversibility of function is amplified if we make use of his brilliantly simple suggestion regarding our classification of emotions. He has suggested that the traditional dichotomies of love–hate, knowledge–ignorance be replaced by positive and negative emotions, plus and minus love, plus and minus hate, plus and minus knowing. Analogously we might think that the opposite of seeing is not blindness but hallucination. Suppose, for instance, in relation to visual perception, we were to imagine that this function could be plotted on coordinate axes, x and y, where the x-axis represented the visualizing, and the y-axis the degree of integration or fragmentation of the image. O, the point of origin, would represent something like hysterical blindness; the artist's vision of the landscape would be the right upper quadrant; the obsessive's preoccupation with detail, the lower right; the paranoid view the upper left and the confusional psychotic's the lower left.

This shift to positive and negative functions is more in accord with the theory of envy as "the spirit that denies", the Satanic element in the personality, the source of cynicism, lies, the operator of the Negative Grid and the architect of Pandemonium. But it takes some stretching of our imagination to cope with such an augmented concept which views, say, the eyes functioning in reverse to project the images of psychic reality as something different from the operation of the omnipotent phantasies of projective identification, as described by Melanie Klein. Perhaps it is closer to the sense given to the term "projection" in traditional psychiatry and as used by Freud, in the sense of "attribution". But that is too intellectual to capture the idea of the visual apparatus actually functioning like a film projector instead of a camera. By "visual apparatus" we do not, of course, mean the eyes alone but the eyes plus the entire central nervous system equipment, at the neurophysiological level, proximal to the operation of mental processes. To draw the analogy correctly we need to envision the equipment of the nervous system available to the mind operating in this way; the eye is the camera, the collicular apparatus develops and projects the image inwards to the occipital area of the cerebrum where the mental apparatus takes over its use. The organ of attention scans, selects, organizes and sets in motion the apparatus of thought for infusing meaning into the image. Perhaps the first step in this infusion of meaning would involve the decision between internal dream image and perception of the external world. At this point the negative of the desire for the truth, minus K, would assert itself to generate the visual hallucination by reversing the direction of the source of image perception (and similarly to generate delusion by reversing the location of the meaning).

The more recent work in dream physiology which revealed the rapid eye-movements (REM) during the dreaming periods of sleep, strongly suggests that the ocular apparatus is behaving during dreaming in a manner identical to its constant scanning activity during waking perception. It is of interest to note that the percentage ratio between REM and non-REM is very different in the adult and the baby, being about 20% in the one and between 5% and 10% in the other. When one considers that the baby sleeps over twice as much as the adult, it would seem that the total dream-time in the twenty-four hours is about the same for the two. This again suggests that the analogy between dream-function and digestive function has more than poetic validity. Humans need time to "chew the cud".

Before we embark on clinical material which, it is hoped, will demonstrate the usefulness of these formulations, both for our understanding of the dream process and what we would like to call its psychopathology – namely hallucination and delusion formation – we must pause a moment to try to grasp the economic significance of such a theory of the reversibility of functions. Melanie Klein's delineation of splitting processes may have introduced a firm structural meaning into the concept of narcissism, thus bringing the idea of the "gang" into view as an organizational principle in the personality, but Bion has gone even a step further. By suggesting that the principles which he discerned as governing group mentality in the outside world may also prevail within the personality, he opened the way for us to recognize evidences of the "tribal" or "political" principle of organization at work internally. The concept of "basic assumption" thinking and the hint that a negative grid may be in operation in the mind have given us the possibility of developing instruments for recognizing and dissecting the mental operations of the political and gang creature within us. But it is also essential to be able to recognize the point of impact of these two sources of irrationality. Where Freud's concept of "mechanism of defence" defined the operation of anxiety modification, Klein's vision of "unconscious phantasy" located it and thus opened the way to a detailed elucidation of these mechanisms. Bion has done the same for us with regard to the principles of organization of the personality as it shifts from moment to moment, from situation to situation, and from one physiological state to another. In this conceptual context it is crucial to view conscious*ness* as the product of an organ of attention which scans and selects the products of alpha-function (Row C of the Grid, unconscious phantasy). It would be to that part of the personality which controls this organ that the power of deploying thought or anti-thought would fall. It corresponds to the situation in the external world where freedom of information is opposed by control of the mass media for purposes of propaganda. Within this framework the concept of control of the organ of consciousness by parts of the personality allied to the good internal objects would have the meaning of "freedom of the internal press". Here would be, *par excellence*, the battle line for sanity and civilized feeling and thought. And here indeed is where we find it in our consulting rooms! Now let us see if clinical experience does in fact demonstrate the utility of these ideas.

Maximillian, called Max, is a nine year old African child attending a school for maladjusted children in London where he receives both enlightened attention from the staff, and psychotherapy from a trainee of the Tavistock Child Psychotherapy Course. Max is a strange little boy, very active and attractive, but virtually mute, ineducable, restless, preoccupied and almost continually hallucinated. The initial months of therapy were taken up with Max filling sheet after sheet with chaotic scribble amidst which there appeared strange little drawings that seem to have been the start of longhand writing and also printed names, mostly of children. He also stared into space, or rather the upper spaces of the room, and it was to this activity that the therapist's attention was often drawn.

As Max's contact with the therapist became less fleeting, he began to assign him certain tasks in relation to a more systematic listing of children's names. For instance, the therapist was supposed to read out the names, or ask specified questions such as, "Who goes on the bus?" or "Where is Sharon?" when her name was left off the list of the children on the school bus or in assembly or in his class. But he also had to answer, "There is no Sharon. Sharon is in Ireland". But clearly "Ireland" meant "up" and Max would immediately begin to scan the upper spaces of the room. Alternatively "no-Anthony" might be at "building school" (boarding school) and up would go Max's eyes, searching. When children's names were not quite known, they might be represented just by a single letter, and the therapist's task was often to spell the names. Once given, the spelling was never again incorrectly written, and the lists became very long and largely correct, both in spelling and in fact, as to the present and absent children.

But Max did not only scan the upper air, he also made writing movements there, pencil in hand. These activities and the limited functions of the therapist seemed interminable until one day two books were introduced by Max, borrowed from the classroom, both about a squirrel, Bushy. In one he was bullied by "Bully", while in the other he was tormented by the "Silly Fly". This tormentor always says, "Watch me", and "Look at me", and "You can't catch me". So it began to appear that the hallucinated objects were connected with the bullying ones, but it was in fact just these bullying children like Anthony who, when he was no-Anthony, was said to be at "building school" up in the air. It was a fact that very aggressive children who disrupted the classes and harassed

119

other smaller children were liable to be sent to the boarding school of the system. Anthony had also been in therapy.

Another phenomenon now presented itself in connection with "no-Anthony" which enabled the therapist to formulate the "Bushy" stories and describe to Max the source of his hallucinations and state of persecution by absent children. In the course of writing "Anthony" there appeared a tendency for the writing to disintegrate into "A" followed by a wiggly line. Then even the "A" lost its shape and became a little round head with a wiggly tail which was followed by searching the upper air. This strongly suggested that the listings which had given way to the "Bushy" stories were enabling Max to "fix" his hallucinated persecutors on the paper, but that they had a tendency to lose their definition and escape from the paper. This made sense of the writing in the air, as a process of catching the persecutor and binding it by its name, to be fixed to the page like a butterfly. It could be recognized in retrospect that these tadpole-like creatures had inhabited the scribble of the initial months of the therapy.

During this stage of the therapy Max's behaviour in the classroom changed noticeably; he became less restless, more attentive and cooperative, much less often hallucinated and more related to the other children and the teacher. Shortly thereafter an incident occurred in which the child was most obscenely abused by a gang of older boys, yet he seemed to take no umbrage. Instead he became much more emotionally attached to his therapist. Material of a transference nature more usual to a child analysis made its appearance. A psycho-analytical therapy had got under way.

The Bionic idiom lends itself almost effortlessly to the elucidation of such material, much as one used jokingly to say that the small children one saw in therapy must have been reading Melanie Klein's *Psychoanalysis of Children*. Maximillian seems to have been tormented with anxiety about "absent children" but was unable to think about the meaning of their absence. Instead these "no" children were expelled from his mental apparatus through his eyes as little homunculi pervading the space in which he lived. So exclusively was his attention directed towards these circulating no-things that he could hardly attend to other aspects of the world. But by enlisting his therapist's capacity to fix them by name on the paper – where the name and the thing-in-itself were quite indistinguishable – the anxiety they engendered by invading his life-space was curtailed for the moment. Yet he had only "fixed" them to the surface of the paper and had not transformed them into representations in his mind, so they tended to struggle free of this bondage and launch themselves once again into his visual field. Only as they took on meaning, began to couple, "fight" and finally to become related to the figures in the world with whom he had begun to interact, albeit masochistically, did the air begin to clear of enemies.

This "fixing" is the process to which our attention is drawn, for it seems so urgent in its inception and so far-reaching in its consequences for Max. We are reminded immediately of Bion's allegory of the contained in search of a container, the "uncertainty cloud" and the "loose reticulum of Dr Jacques", as he puckishly calls it. There can be little doubt that Max was very menaced by these circulating objects and that the little tadpole or spermatozoalike creatures held some dire threat for him. If Karen or Duncan could become "no-" children, might not Max as well be transformed into a flying homunculus in someone else's visual field? The likeness to ideas of ghosts and spirits would not be too fanciful a construction to put upon a process in the mind of a child raised in a family still permeated with tribal culture. But then again we are putting forward a theory of the mind which includes the possibility of a "tribal" level of mentality even in the most sophisticated personalities.

Is what we have called "fixing" the same as Bion's reference to "binding" as being the function of "naming"? We are concerned with the geographic location of the object while he is perhaps more concerned with the binding of the object to an epistemological container into which meaning may then be poured. But we have suggested that the fixing of the geography may indeed be the first step in the operation of alpha-function and the point at which the reversing of alpha-function produces not only the "beta-elements with traces of ego and super-ego" but also the reversal of direction of the function of the perceptual apparatus. Perhaps our next clinical example will carry the argument a step further towards persuasion, since it seems to suggest a process similar to Max's, but operating on a dream-figure to transform it into a waking hallucination.

Abdul is an eighteen year old Indian youth, well-built and intelligent, from a devout Moslem family, with two younger sisters. Since coming to this country three years ago he has grown progressively withdrawn, churlish, demanding and aggressive, unable to continue his education. His days are spent increasingly preoccupied with day-dreams and imaginary figures, such as a "brother-in-law" named Arnold and others which are easily recognized by him as parts of himself. The day-dreams cannot confidently be distinguished from events in the outside world, not so much at the moment as in retrospect. Certainly his day-dream world is more vivid to him than the constricted contact with external reality, which had become limited to the family and home until he came into analysis with a child psychotherapist five months earlier.

To a mid-week session he brought this dream: *I was watching a football match which seemed to be turning into a fight between the two teams. The spectators, all children and young people, including my sister and two boys whom I recognized from unhappy school days, ran into a dark hall. A boy turned on a projector and showed a fragment of the match but the machine broke down. The boy was humorous about it. Then someone turned on me and called me "a killer", and then a mad boy* (the patient's imaginary brother-in-law Arnold) *came up and said, "My daddy says you can teach me karate".*

Further associations and description indicated that for the first time his day-dream world had entered into his dreams. Arnold has been getting madder recently in his day-dreams, while still rather nice. In the dream the patient had felt lost among other people, not "knowing his place". The boy's humorous response to the projector breaking down struck him as contrasting with the rage and impulse to strike his mother that he had felt yesterday when she had incorrectly videoed a TV programme for him when he was away at analysis. It was not clear if this programme was connected with Arnold's recent scheme for forging billions in U.S. currency in order to alter or wreck the capitalist economy and thus benefit the poor; the patient thought that Arnold's motives were neither political nor altruistic but more for his own amusement. It is connected with the printing machinery at his home used by the father in his work; it also has some link to the payment for the analysis which comes from a family Trust.

Five months of analysis seem to have brought this adolescent, struggling with a new culture, back from the brink of a serious psychotic breakdown. He has grasped at the analysis eagerly and cooperated well, being confiding, attentive and even courageous in facing humiliation and shame about his feelings and preoccupations. We appear to have caught him in the moment of stepping back from the attraction of delusion and hallucination, recapturing, as it were, his sense of an internal dream-world. The critical point of the dream is the moment when the football game threatens to break down into a fight, linked with his almost striking his mother in rage about the video error. We see that he is able to pull back from this impulse by what is represented in the dream as the spectators running into a dark hall where a fragment of the match was to be projected on a screen. This, I would suggest, is a representation of the newly recovered capacity to dream, and therefore to think, about the near-delusional system of his day-dreams.

But notice what happens: the machine breaks down and the

madness begins to assert itself again – in the form of the patient being called "a killer" and the mad Arnold soliciting karate lessons. This seems to have happened despite the boy-projectionist treating the break-down humorously. The delicate balance between dream and thought on the one hand, and delusion and hallucination on the other seems strongly suggested. The outbreak of violence, in his mind as on the football field of the dream is clearly the threatening possibility, basically violence towards his mother if she does not function as his apparatus of thought represented by the video machine she is meant to operate for him in his absence. We might paraphrase the situation as follows:

> When I am watching two people having an intense relationship with one another, the excitement that it arouses in me is indistinguishable from destructive violence in myself and in the couple. It is necessary to withdraw into sleep and try to have a dream in order to be able to discover the meaning of this experience. But if my internal mother and her video-breast break down, then I cannot dream or think and am awakened with violent impulses. (The dream in fact awakened the patient at 1:30 in the morning.)

The transference significance of the dream is strikingly suggested by the material of Arnold's plan for counterfeiting, and also by the impact upon the patient of the recent Easter break in the analysis. His dependence upon the analyst to help him to think about his experiences centres, at this point, on forestalling the tendency for these experiences to be agglomerated, as Bion would say, into a mass of beta-elements forming a pseudo-contact barrier of day-dream, verging on delusion and hallucination. It can be said with fair confidence that this is the main accomplishment of the five months of analysis, namely the establishment of dependence upon the therapist to perform the thinking functions, since his internal mother and her video–apparatus–breast breaks down under his stressful demand.

PART C

THE PRACTICE OF DREAM
INVESTIGATION

IX

The Borderland between Dreams and Actions

If we are to be faithful to the model of the mind defined by the extended metapsychology of Klein and Bion, we must assume that the dream process is the foundation not only of our view-of-the-world, and therefore of mood, but also that every dream is an attempt to solve a conflict which, while primarily an internal world matter, has implications for behaviour in the outside world. It is clear that individuals differ widely in their capacity to utilize thought as a mediator between impulse and action; some indeed seem to overreach its utility and replace action by thought, so that impulse finds no expression in the outside world. From that point of view the aim of action to modify the external world so that it more aptly meets the individual's requirements, or at least his desires, is lost in internal world modification.

In understanding the place of dreams in our lives, or rather the relation between our dream life and our total life-process, we need to address ourselves to both aspects of this problem – denial of psychic reality with its reliance on experimental action, and retreat from external reality with its many forms of withdrawal. Somewhere in between the two ends of the spectrum of the mediation by thought between impulse and action, lies the realm of art-science where thought is content to act in the service of knowledge of the outside world without necessarily intending its modification. There is good reason to think that love-making in its most developed form belongs to this art-science area. I have chosen this middle ground between acting-out and withdrawal, between excessive and inadequate transformation of dream-life into action, as the most fruitful area for investigation of the problem. But what, in fact, is the problem?

In this chapter I address myself mainly to the technical problems in the practice of analysis. In what way does the analysis of dreams enable us to help the patient to pursue the evolution of the transference experience without either being plunged into acting-out or driven into withdrawal in his life outside the consulting room? Another useful way of stating the problem would be this: how can we have an experience of the transference-countertransference with a patient without the process escaping from the containment of the analytic situation for either member? "He no longer thought of it as treatment. The reasons he went to analysis had vanished years ago; it was the way he lived." (A. Alvarez, *Life after Marriage* Macmillan, London, 1982).

This type of transformation from a treatment to a way of life can be duplicated in the analyst whose relationships in his consulting room gradually become not merely the most intimate, but the only intimate ones in his life.

First I will illustrate by some clinical material this area of the art–science–love-making spectrum of this borderland between dream and action, and then return to the discussion of the technical problem.

A scientist from abroad, residing in London for a year's sabbatical in order to finish a book, came to analysis in November after three sterile months in which he had hardly put pen to paper. He had had extensive analysis in his native country which he felt had enabled him to marry and start a family; now a second child was wanted but his sexual impulse was dwindling again, despite a powerful conscious attraction to his wife and a deep desire for a little girl to complete the family constellation. He strongly suspected that both areas involved an inhibition of creativity with a common basis.

From the beginning of the therapy, four times per week, his excellent cooperation was marked by a special feature – he talked not only with his tongue but with his hands in a most eloquent combination. The theatrical performance with which his gestures amplified and clarified his inadequately expressive way of speaking was most impressive. In no way were his movements cultural expressions of emotion, but rather reminded me of the "tiny theatre in the lap" which elective mute children often create. So much a part of his communication system did these gestures seem to be, that it did not occur to me to think of them as a phenomenon to be investigated, although I was aware that by this means he induced me to watch continually (as well as listen) which is not my custom. I am more in the habit of closing my eyes while listening, with periodic monitoring of the patient's posture or his facial expressions as seen on the side of his face from my diagonal orientation to the couch.

The first holiday break at Christmas brought him a surprisingly sharp experience of longing for the analysis, which seemed to link strongly with his father's death. But he also had a respite from his writing inhibition with good accomplishment. Yet his wife was not pregnant nor was his potency much augmented. The following term's work was rich and interesting to us both but somehow lacked direction, and the approach to the Easter break was without tension. He had planned a trip to Scotland with his wife and child, which was carried out with great enjoyment, both the writing and analysis being far from his mind – in contrast to the Christmas break.

When he returned to analysis in January he experienced great difficulty in resuming his engagement to the work, until he produced a dream which, for the first time, drew our attention to the role of his hands in the analysis. He dreamed that *he was on holiday, in his car which was parked. As he found himself unable to start it because of a flat battery, he required someone to push him. A man dressed like a mechanic appeared and pushed him out of his parking place backwards, telling him to put the gears in reverse in order to start the motor. In fact this mechanic gave him a mighty shove and the motor started, but he woke at this point in a great state of anxiety that he had run over his child.*

This was our first indication that his "mechanic" hands had anything to do with what he had often complained of in his writing, namely of mechanistic modes of thought curtailing more imaginative flight and abstraction. But it also suggested that the division of labour between tongue and hand in his communications in the analysis might impoverish rather than enrich their content. While his hands seemed to be such a great help in overcoming some verbal inhibition (the stalled motor due to the flat battery), the mechanical drama which they produced perhaps pushed his thought in a retrograde direction which threatened to destroy what had already been created in his mind rather than to restore his flagging creativity.

We were both so impressed by this dream, and he by the severe charge of anxiety with which it had awakened him, that he decided that his hands should be immobilized by his lying on them. The urgency of the last few months available for analysis seemed to justify this unusual procedure. The result was striking. The colourfulness and fluidity of his talking fairly leaped ahead and the analysis sprang to life again. So did his writing, but not his sexual life – to his great disappointment. This had to wait for its clarification by another dream almost at the eleventh hour: *He was riding his bicycle with his child on the little seat behind him, but the little boy was complaining of his father's maltreatment of the cycle. Not only was he going too fast but he was also abusing the handlebars. He was turning them up.* (Here he had great difficulty in conveying his meaning to me and his hands escaped from beneath him to make the gesture: hands holding the bars horizontally, palms upwards, then a sharp movement to bring the hands together in the vertical position.) The reference to the Hollywood cliché for submarine warfare was unmistakable and we both recognized it. The captain peers through the periscope; the enemy ship appears in the cross-hairs; he orders, "Fire one", and folds the scope handles up, thus lowering the periscope.

He immediately associated to the name of an actor playing the captain of a particular film from his childhood. He fell silent, thoughtful, then proceeded himself to investigate the significance of this image for his sexual life. He realized that so long as he does not put his hands under his partner's buttocks in intercourse he has good control of his ejaculation, but that the urge to do so is very great, and the loss of control almost immediate. The implied link with the "mechanic" dream was apparent; here again his hands interfered in his love relationships and pushed him in the direction of sado-masochism, torpedoing the babies as well as running over them. The regression to anal sadism seemed implicit.

This clinical example, which weds sexual love and artistic creativity so neatly, should also serve as a paradigm of the relation between dream-life and action in the outside world, action meant to participate in the creativity of the world rather than to modify the world to meet the invididual's needs or desires. If we examine it in detail it should reveal to us some of the secrets of the craftsmanship we are seeking to develop.

The first problem to which our attention is drawn is the distinction between acting-out and acting-in in the transference. The "mechanic" dream was the fruit of investigation of a piece of acting-out which made the Easter break into *his* family holiday in order to forestall a repetition of the separation reaction, related to the pain of his mourning for his father, which had occurred at Christmas. Its investigation, or perhaps merely its occurrence, propelled the stalled analysis once again in a useful direction. It brought to my attention something that I should perhaps have recognized as a phenomenon for investigation much earlier – his hand activities. I would plead in mitigation such factors as the urgency of the situation, due to the closed-ended nature of our working arrangement, perhaps feeling comforted to be in the same dock with the Melanie Klein of the *Narrative* with its various forgivable technical sins. But I think the truth would be that in the countertransference, I shared with my patient both his admiration for, and gratitude towards, these "mechanic" hands.

Perhaps a more important aspect of the problem lies at a conceptual level, namely a too limited idea of the scope of the technical concept, "acting-in the transference". Perhaps it has been taken too much merely as a geographic differentiation from acting-out, or as a formulation for the differentiation between action and communication in the consulting room or playroom. Material of this sort reminds one of the need to remember that, as I have discussed at some length earlier, an important distinction needs to be made between the vocalization of the patient (the song-and-dance level at which projective identificatory methods are employed to communicate states of mind) and the verbal level with its essential dependence on the lexical means of communicating information, information in this case about the state of mind and its content.

This broader view of acting-in the transference is in fact implicit in our clinical work and in the tacit acceptance of this mode of communication by direct emotional impingement on the counter-transference. Acting-out, on the other hand, most analysts would view as undesirable, to be forestalled by alert interpretation whenever possible. Where it cannot thus be forestalled, its sub-sequent investigation can at least be facilitated by pre-emptive in-terpretation, when the material makes this possible. But acting-in which stays within the geographic limits of the analytic situation and neither threatens the safety of the working couple nor the prerogatives of the other patients, is fundamentally acceptable, if not always bearable.

In the few hours per week in which the teeming process of the transference-countertransference unfolds itself, there is not time to pay attention to everything that would reasonably come under the umbrella of this extended concept of acting-in. Our technical problem is not merely the recognition of the existence of these idiosyncratic factors of personality functioning (in the patient and in ourselves as we respond individually to them) but in recognizing when a particular factor has become significant and requires in-vestigation because it has begun to function as an obstacle (I will not say "resistance") to the investigation in train.

The material presented illustrates the essential role that dream investigation plays in this process of location. But, of course, it is self-idealizing to think that one catches the reference as soon as it appears. In fact, having caught this reference to the patient's hands in the "mechanic" dream, I could not help but realize that it could be recognized in retrospect in previous ones but had pas-sed unnoticed at the time.

Another factor regarding the atmosphere of the consulting room also needs attention. It is very difficult for the patient to allow himself to be swept away by the emotionality of the transfer-ence and its phenomenology if he is constantly reminded of the presence of the analyst as an observer, rather than merely as an auditor. Not that he does not really know and expect the analyst to be observing, but the constant reminder of it by comments on his behaviour has a signally inhibiting influence on his relaxation. For this reason I am seldom willing to comment on a patient's action which may strike me as likely to be carrying a load of phan-tasy until I am in a position to suggest some significance for it on the basis of collateral material. Here again, nothing presents such rich suggestiveness for integration with a meaningful action as a dream which contains a reference to it – or at least seems to. The

obvious fact that the analyst has been thinking, has himself inter-
posed thought between impulse and action in regard to the observation, takes away from the communication to the patient the persecutory sting of being under scrutiny.

   In closing this chapter it might be well to attempt at least some
enquiry into the theoretical as well as the technical problem concerning the borderland between dreams and actions in the outside
world. Modern literature has seized hold of the thesis, which
Joseph first and Prospero later so clearly proclaimed, that our
dreams are the foundation of our actions in the outside world in
the area of our passionate concerns (as distinct from our animal
needs and our social adjustments). Can psycho-analytical experience of dream investigation tell us anything compelling regarding
the structure of this spectrum that ranges from unreflective experimental action to states of withdrawal and delusion? Bion has
probably given us the conceptual equipment with which to approach the problem and has even gone some distance himself in
answering it at one end of the spectrum with his conception of
reality testing by multiplication of vertices. Or does this multiplication of our imaginative capacity really belong to this middle
ground of the lover–artist–scientist? I would be inclined to think
so and the material of our scientist would seem to bear this out. If
this is the case, then the problem of the spectrum would be considerably reduced. We could restate it as the problem of impoverished imagination. Gide has said pungently that people who
pride themselves on their self-control are in fact suffering from
poverty of imagination. Experience in analysis certainly bears this
out, for the whole range of character disturbance based on denial
of psychic reality is founded on it. But the withdrawn person and
the deluded person do not seem to be impoverished, but rather to
be suffering from a superfluity in this area of imagination.

   On the other hand, a little study like Gogol's *Diary of a Madman*
suggests the same thesis that Bion's concept of the Basic Assumption Group outlines, namely the constriction amounting to
mindlessness of the *idée fixe* or the Basic Assumption. Contact with
dream-life seems the antidote to the excursion of the spectrum in
either direction. We must live our dream-life, for it *is* our imagination. Sometimes a patient presents us with a dream that we wish
we could have had ourselves. One such, which I shall never forget,
came at the end of the analysis of a young writer at the time that
he was writing the book which eventually established his reputa-
tion and, incidentally, earned him a fortune. In the dream he was
sitting at his typewriter in a little booth on whose walls his name
was written repeatedly and he had on earphones, taking dictation,
like Milton's "unpremeditated verse".

X

Dream-exploration and Dream-analysis

As a science, psycho-analysis is committed to the discovery of the truth about the events in our own minds and also the truth about our own actions. To make public either of these clearly requires the overcoming of an immense anxiety, both persecutory and depressive. What we reveal to the "group" is probably the most terrifying; what hostage we give to our "enemies" is the most intimidating; but what we reveal to our "siblings" threatens to demonstrate the disparity of our internal objects and thus that we are "foster-" brothers and sisters at best. The loneliness consequent upon this realization is surely one of the great deterrents to revelation to colleagues of our actual behaviour in our consulting rooms. But first of all it deters us from discovering what we in fact do, as against what we think we do, wish we did, feel we ought to do or aspire to do. What follows is an attempt to report the monitoring of my work with my patients' dreams and cannot be taken as a recommended method for anyone else. Its crudeness as a statement when compared with the great intricacy of what actually happens will immediately be apparent, but it is the best I can do at the moment. It may help other analysts to monitor and discover what they in fact do; it is of no importance whether this turns out to be similar or different from what I am able to report.

There is no doubt in my mind that I feel pleasure and relief when a patient reports a dream, for I feel that he is "playing the game on my home ground", so to speak. And, correspondingly, I know that I begin to become uneasy about the nature of the work I have been doing if it fails to elicit dream-material over a protracted period. This is modified in the case of patients who maintain a strong denial of psychic reality and thus a consistent reluctance to come into contact with the dream-life they are leading. I feel that to tell a dream is an act of great confidentiality and inherent truthfulness, made possible by the narrator's option to distance himself from the emotional cyclone of the dream according to the requirements of his comfort. Consequently the problem of tactfulness and modulation of the dreamer's mental pain in relating it has already been at least half done for me – a great aid to relaxation.

Furthermore I feel confident when a dream is being reported that I am being given the means for discerning how the work of the previous session has been "digested". From the point of view of the necessity in analytical work of following the continuity of the process, my task of recognizing errors of all sorts is made easier, whether these be errors of comprehension, of presentation, of modulating the setting or of breaches of technique. One consequence is a feeling of gratitude to the patient, which in many ways, as a countertransference experience, parallels the patient's transference feeling of presenting a gift, a deed of gratitude, while at the same time he is asking for more of the attention and attempts at understanding which are the food-for-thought of the analytical dependence with its infantile neediness.

In listening to a dream I note that I always close my eyes, apparently the better to follow the image that the patient's description is evoking in my mind. This makes it possible to note the areas of vagueness or ambiguity in that description, facilitating enquiry into the details, often of the setting (one might say "stage-setting") of the dream, for the patient is usually more absorbed in the narrative aspects and description of the emotionality. This filling out of the scene, with set and costumes, also throws up associational material from the patient in his own attempts to transform into verbal language the visual language of the dream itself. Thus it often happens that the cooperative work between analyst and analysand, in this publication of the dream experience, produces an interweaving of dream and associations which must then be sorted out before any systematic exploration of the dream can be undertaken.

I find myself hesitating over this expression "systematic exploration", wondering if it is perhaps too pompous a description of what actually takes place. I myself, and I think most of my patients, find the exploring and analysis of dreams something of a game, during which the heat of the transference-countertransference is held in abeyance, partly by the patient's own "distancing" with regard to the dream as life-experience, but also surely partly because of my own suspension of what Bion calls "memory and desire". The "fun" of this great game which Freud invented and played so well is certainly to some extent intellectual, puzzle-solving, like his jig-saw analogy. But like sport, relaxation is certainly a necessary state of mind for skilled "play". It has something of the quality of the "opening moves" in chess or bridge, and the tension does not assert itself until the vague outlines of the pattern of the game begin to emerge. This is often heralded by the analyst's first shy approach to interpretive comment; and I notice, as the years go by, that my work tends to prolong this pleasant phase of exploration and delay the interpretative move. Perhaps this is also strengthened by a growing tendency to wait for something to emerge in the intuitive grasp of the dream that carries an emotional charge of excitement; I consider this as essentially aesthetic, something to do with appreciating the formal and compositional aspects of the dream as an event of theatrical proportions.

But often the exploration of the dream does not evoke any such intuitive grasp and excitement. Then a sense of disappointment can often be noted in the patient, coupled with uneasiness. Was the analyst asleep? Did his attention stray? Is he not well, or fatigued – or losing interest? These same questions appear in the countertransference in a very distressing way that seems to centre its attention on the "eyes-closed" way of listening. I think this is because the split in one's attention which takes place at that time, looking inward at the image forming while listening to the patient's account, threatens the analyst more than usually with confusion. He finds himself uncertain, for instance, of the patient's precise words because the image that forms itself in his mind is also frequently immediately described verbally within himself, and these two sets of description – the patient's primary one and the analyst's secondary one – do not necessarily tally. Associations of one's own, either from previous material from the patient or worse still from other patients' or one's own personal experience, also crowd into the perimeter of the field of attention. This crowding of one's mental field tends to begin to pulsate with confusion that is somehow juxtaposed to the mounting excitement when an interpretive intuition is forming. The pleasant game of exploration now begins to yield place to growing unrest and distress in the analyst, and the atmosphere of the consulting room can become thick with anxious expectation and incipient disappointment. This is certainly a moment when Bion's "Column 2" becomes very real; that is, the tendency to make statements that are known to be false in order to hide one's ignorance from oneself and the patient. I find that it is my custom – one could hardly call it "technique" – to start talking, just reviewing the material, sorting out with the patient the text of the dream, the associations, the links with previous material, waiting for something to happen in my mind but holding the situation in a quiet state to give my mind space and time to work. Once interpretive notions begin to form and the confusion gives way to excitement, cooperative work with the patient commences again. But now it is a tense situation, anxiety and resistance are incipient, and the easeful time afforded by the patient's distancing is at an end.

The phrase "intrepretive notions" I use to describe the vagueness with which the formulation of a dream begins to emerge. I notice that as the excitement of comprehension and a sense of being in the presence of an aesthetic object grows, the tendency to talk for the purpose of holding the situation suspended gives way to a different type of talking in which the patient is less inclined to join until he is an experienced dream-interpreter himself. This type of talking has a spiral feel to it, circling about in the material, uttering interpretive notions, waiting a moment for some response, going on to another aspect and notion, and so on, until a fabric of interpretation begins to weave itself together. Of course all this is lost when a paper is written, for the marshalling of the material for exposition requires that the interpretation follow "as the night the day", effortlessly, unforced, dovetailed. In the consulting room it is not that way at all; nor does it necessarily take place in a single session, for a rich dream is constantly being retrospectively lit up in one aspect or another by the material and events of following sessions.

I am not fond of the word "interpretation" for this process of formulation, as it suggests that some increment of meaning has been added by the analyst. "Formulation" is probably better, since the process – in my view, which is after all the central thesis of this book – is one of transformation from one symbolic form to another, from largely visual to verbal language. Far from an increment of meaning, an impoverishment is surely imposed by this process; the "poetic diction" of the dream is reduced to the prose of psycho-analese. In certain hands – a Freud's or a Bion's – this jargon may be raised to a poetic level; it may sometimes happen at lyrical moments in one's own consulting room. But it is not generally the case.

The formulation of a dream is only the foundation of the interpretive work. The heavier task, in which the analyst is alone with his capacity for constructive thought and generally deserted by his intuition except at moments of inspiration, is the task of discerning the significance of a particular dream. For some analysts this means particularly its reference to the transference process, for others its contribution to the reconstruction – for a few it means both. That aspect of the work with dreams belongs to a volume of psycho-analytical method and must be put aside here.

What more can we say about formulation? While admitting that most formulations end up as prose, this need not deter us from striving to match the poetic diction of the dream as an aesthetic object, with a worthy transformation into verbal language, a poetry of our own. Our first striving is towards order, for the material impinges on us as analysts in just as confusing and "meaningless" a way as it does on the waking dreamer himself – probably more so. But this striving is not to put order into the chaos of the dream, for that has its own order. Rather we seek to put order into the confusion in our own minds, into the image of the dreamer's communication of his own recollection, surrounded now with associations, links to previous material, budding interpretive notions, and various extraneous – or are they? – bits of private ideas. All this is pervaded by the ineffable emotional atmosphere, first of the telling of the dream, later of the mounting anxiety and resistance of the patient confronting the excitement of the analyst.

How does it happen? I have described at a purely external level the behaviour that I note in myself, this talking around the material, voicing bits of interpretive notion, etc. But what goes on inside? Is there a describable order of events, an internal logic of the process? The most interesting approach to this question would need two phases: first I would have to produce my general retro- and intro-spective impression; then I would have to lay this chapter aside and wait for an experience in the consulting room to investigate "hot"; then we will see how the two impressions match. What then of my general retrospective impression?

I do not think of it as an especially orderly experience. The most vivid impression, as I have said, is one of struggling out of the rather dozy confusion as the excitement mounts and the patient's anxiety begins to fill the room with expectation. One thing is clear: I deal with the clarified image of the patient's dream as my own dream and delve into it exactly as I might into my own dream on awakening. My own tendency to view the matter in theatrical terms seems to produce a kind of jounalistic, theatre critic response. There is a "story" and sometimes a "plot", as E.M. Forster would distinguish them. And enmeshed in this story and plot there is a cast of characters, some good, some bad, some old, some young, male and female, some clearly parts of the self, some clearly alienated as objects. And there is the stage setting, whose reference to the geography of psychic life is often clearly indicated in the patient's mode of presentation.

Let us go back to the "Miss Spoonerism" dream. The theatrical presentation brought to view was a clear one: a gathering of adults presided over by famous and beautiful parents was being intruded upon by a little boy who yearned for his mother's white body (the car), but his confusion between wanting her breasts (front garden) for nourishment and desiring her buttocks (back garden) for sexual possession made him furtive and uneasy, uncertain of his welcome (presumably to the parental bedroom), inclined to avert his gaze from such beauty so that his lust should not be manifest. When questioned about his reasons for coming into their room he was inclined to lie (to say that he needed to go to the toilet, for instance). It is a scene that any child might participate in, say at the age of three, with regard to the parental bedroom, repeated at later ages when the parents entertain guests in the evening. Rather banal so far.

To return to the process of formulation: having recognized the dramatic scene and its infantile reference, certain features begin to emerge which are not "covered" by the simple narrative. They seem mystifying, even nonsensical, sometimes trivial, like the little pavilion that was being used as a First Aid Station. But clearly the narrative formulation does not cover them and a more creative intuition is called for. At this point I find that I may, if no interpretive notion occurs, ask for more detailed description of these "uncovered" details. But in the case of the little pavilion–First Aid Station, it was coupled with the death of Miss Spoonerism, so the line of investigation went in that direction and brought forth the blushing crow- crushing blow association.

This phase of the formulating process may bear no immediate fruit. The dream can be put aside with some degree of disappointment, but can be returned to in future sessions if new light is shed on the un-covered facets. Clearly I feel, in formulating the dream, that "cover" is essential for a satisfying conception, where "satisfying" probably means "in the aesthetic realm". I occasionally feel stunned by the beauty of a formulation, and no less rarely a patient can also have this experience. Although it is relatively rare, it is nonetheless so impressive an experience that I am convinced that this aesthetic element is crucial to the development of any sense of conviction about the "correctness" of the formulation. A treacherous word, "correct"; what meaning can we give it that does not have the penumbra of exclusiveness? We could, for instance, mean no more than "valid" or "useful viewpoint" or "tenable hypothesis". Or just "interesting", the most mysterious word of all. But certainly we do not mean *the* correct formulation, only *a* correct formulation.

Once a "satisfying" formulation that "covers" has been reached and some sense of aesthetic has arisen, the phase of formulation seems to come to an end and the work of discerning the significance of the dream commences.

Before going on to try to investigate the processes whereby the formulation of a dream is raised to the level of interpretation by means of an investigation of its significance for the transference or reconstruction, or both, it would seem opportune to undertake the second phase of this description, the "hot" example. Two months after writing the previous section I selected a dream, partly because it seemed relatively simple once solved but quite mysterious to begin with. Also I had some time to make notes and knew that I would be able to record it more fully in the evening.

Later still I undertook to annotate the session surrounding the dream with an account of the processes in my mind which resulted in the questions, comments, and finally the formulation that I proposed.

The session was on a Thursday evening, late in September, the twentieth month of this young man's five-times-a-week analysis. Although he had been a frequent reporter of dreams in the early months of analysis they had become rather rare later on. In fact, in the four weeks since the summer break he had only been able to report one (in the first week) until the present example. This had been a disappointment to him since he had found the discussion of dreams the most enlightening part of the work I could do for him. Five or six dreams already formed the landmarks of the analytical progress which, up to this point, had been satisfactory to patient and analyst alike.

P. I had a dream last night which I forgot until a minute ago. *It was a street in Australia, up and down, hilly. I was waiting at a cross-roads, in the middle of the minor road, with my suitcase resting on one of those lumps of metal – they probably don't have them any more – when a man on a bicycle-like contraption came along. When I saw him I automatically grimaced, but when he stopped a hundred yards on I realized it was my transport. It had four white wire baskets, on either side, front and back, and I was meant to ride on the front right one. There was someone, a Southern Irishman, in the left side already and it was necessary for me to put my foot on the foot-rest of his basket – they seemed to be called "modules" – while he put his foot on mine.* (silence) That is all I can remember.

We had been occupied recently with his unfriendliness to the other students at school, which he had resumed after a three year break following a poor performance at A-levels and a year in Australia during which he had a breakdown. The dream clearly related to "getting back" from Australia, back from being cut off from intimate relationships. His "automatic" unfriendliness is a great obstacle, being accompanied by contemptuous thoughts and irritability. But at this point I could not get a clear image of the dream nor did any configuration known in the analysis come to my mind. I thought the "cross"-road referred to his mood when waiting at the weekends, which he still finds empty and difficult, being without friends and unable to participate in the family life of the people with whom he lodges.

A. The grimace?

P. My usual, disdain or contempt, I suppose.

A. And the bicycle-like contraption?

P. A bicycle, I guess, really. Like the Moulton that is outside when I leave here in the mornings. I don't know why they were called 'modules' in the dream or maybe 'nodules'. No, 'modules'. Space vehicles, computer components?

A. The Paris airport?

P. Oh, yes. I got stuck there on the way back from Australia. I had two suitcases and my French horn and they lost the two cases – I didn't trust them with the horn. The one in the dream is smaller than those two. I was pleased, thinking I'd buy new clothes, that I'd gather old receipts and get the money from the airline But the cases turned up two weeks later in my room. I guess my brother had received them and put them there. I was too weak to carry anything but the horn, and so thin. (silence) I was just thinking about how I laughed when I first heard about this boxer who is in a coma after six days and six hours on the operating table. But it was because I was not thinking of him but of the great row there

I needed to establish the mood, for he has many grimaces, most of which seem to be defensive postures against the expectation of unfriendliness or contempt from others on the grounds of his non-existent "fatness". It is characteristic to equivocate his descriptions and so it is necessary to fix the meaning by such questions. He knows that the Moulton belongs to a girl who sees my wife and we both know that jealousy and competitiveness with his siblings, bi-sexual in its orientation, is a central theme. I remembered something of his account of the trip back from Australia and having to wait at the Paris Airport – but I was confusing "module" with "satellite". However, it seemed to be the right track and tapped a line of association. I could now see that the dream had something to do with waiting, being too weak to protect his internal objects (the two cases) and being ready to give them up in exchange for feelings of triumph and superiority. But he does cling to something aesthetic (the horn, perhaps the mother's voice if not the full experience of the breast). This much was already established and I could see at this point the emotive background of the dream. The conflict between tender and heartless attitudes towards himself was also clearly indicated by the "boxer" material, for he has been the "hitting" one of the family ever would be now about boxing being unsafe. Later when I thought of *him* and how sad it was also, I still thought "they won't find much to work with inside his head", thinking of how unintelligent and selfish he seemed, could hardly put a sentence together and talked with such childish gratitude of his parents.

A. The automatic inhumanity of the grimace in the dream, immediate ridicule and contempt that displaces humane feelings, seems to be connected with yesterday's material of your rows with your lady boss in Australia when she did not cater for you as you were accustomed to mother doing at home. Also it links to our discussion of your unfriendliness to your fellow students.

P. I guess so. Yes, I was just now remembering how contemptuous I felt of the teacher explaining such simple things as analogies, but really he did it well and I could not have given as good an explanation if he had asked me, although I know perfectly well what an analogy is.

A. Could we go back to the "lump of metal" in the road. I don't get a clear image of it.

since he outgrew his father and his elder brother in stature.

I now began to feel confident that the figure on the bicycle-like contraption was myself and the six hours on the operating table corresponded to the analysis. Clearly he is afraid that his mind is childish and empty of talents, that all his intelligence is squandered in his habitual pose as the critic of other people's actions. But this was all well-known and did not seem to be the central theme of the dream but rather its background. Passivity in relation to the mother, which produced the massive state of withdrawal into projective identification of his breakdown state, is still a mystery to me, as it manifests itself as a paralysis of interest and initiative. Now that he is back at his studies his capacity to work is continually threatened by this recurring paralysis.

A bell suddenly rang in my head. The scene in the dream in which he is standing with his case resting on the "lump of metal" places him and the lump in an analogous relation to one another. I turn my attention to this item.

P. They have them in the middle at the junctions with main roads, painted yellow and standing up to keep people from cutting the corner. Stupid things.

A. Do you feel critical because they are, in effect, actions to punish cornercutters rather than communications?

P. Yes, they are unnecessary. It is all in the Highway Code. We have white lines lines and "Give Way" signs.

A. Then it sounds as if there is an analogy here, between the "lump" that is ready to punish the 'cornercutter' and your grimace. You are ready to punish this man on the "bicycle-like contraption" because you expect him to be unfriendly and "cut" or ignore you.

P. (silence) The "module" baskets were a bit like the baskets on the beds in the hospital for holding infusion bottles.

A. Perhaps you mean the bottles for collecting urine from catheterized patients.

P. Oh, yes, of course. Or the four together would be like the carts the cleaners wheel about for collecting refuse.

It now began to hang together. I had not heard previously of the yellow colour and wondered about the role of cowardice in this defensive posture. But it also seemed to me that the central theme of action versus communication in human relations was shining through the dream. This seemed to link with the boxer's incapacity to "put a sentence together" and his own tendency to tyrannize over his family by outbreaks of violence or threats of it. I was wondering now about the hundred yards that it took the man on the bicycle-contraption to stop to pick up the patient. Clearly he must have at first taken the patient's posture as an indicator that he was not wanting transportation. I was also thinking that the "cutting corners" had some reference to ambition and impatience, both of which play an important role in the ease with which the patient becomes discouraged. This adds to his feelings of worthlessness and certainly coming into analysis had seemed a humiliation to him to begin with, hence the association to "refuse collecting". The confusion here between "infusion bottle" and "urine bottle" seemed therefore to link with his uncertainty in the transference between dumping the refuse of his mind into me as against infusing me with his brilliant criticisms of the world about us.

A. So this Moulton-Meltzer contraption for collecting your refuse seems to have stopped for you, either despite your grimace or perhaps because it recognized the grimace as a manifestation of some blow to your mind, as you, like the boxer, were so skinny and helpless when you returned from Australia in your breakdown. It may link with that aggressive little boy in that dream who was expelled from the ramshackle maternity hospital and was so irate that he went about knocking everyone out.

P. I suppose he'll just be a vegetable if he survives. Everyone used to laugh at him. He'd been a gravedigger. I guess I *have* always been deferred to in the family, mostly because I shout and hit, but also because I was considered for some reason to be the brightest of the children.

A. So perhaps even the yellow colour fits into the analogy between you and the lump of metal, that there is some cowardice involved in the inhumane behaviour that demands to be deferred to, for it takes some courage to make friendly advances, to say "please" when you want something because you might be rebuffed or refused if you communicate,

The dream has now taken on a clear narrative structure in my mind, linking with the recent sessions as well as with the history of the patient's illness and his development in the family. His poor performance at A-levels had been a terrible blow, although not completely unexpected because he had ceased to be able to study for at least six months before the exams. He had lost weight through being unable to allow himself food in Australia until he was so weak he could hardly stand. The first year of analysis had released him from this withdrawn state but also confronted him with the great difficulty of life in the outside world, his resentment of which has been the theme of this landmark dream of the "irate little boy". He had almost dug his own grave indeed and the fear of humiliation assumed the leading anxiety, in his relation to people, that he'd be variously thought to be fat, childish, stupid, useless, ignorant, sexless.

So now it was possible to begin to explore the significance of the dream for the immediate transference situation. This seemed to me to centre on his basic attitude towards the analysis and towards financial dependence on his family now that he was returning to his education and needed their help once again. I had an idea that the "foot on each other's foot-rest" had a very important

143

but you take no risk if you act in an automatic, threatening and inhumane way. The Irishman already there in the basket would be your elder brother and the man I see before you in the early morning. But what is this business about having a foot on each other's foot-rest?

P. (silence) It was terrible to see him standing there, his arms at his side when he was being hit, and then went down striking his head. He looked so skinny and helpless, a bantamweight. He had been winning against the champion and then seemed to fold up once he was knocked down in the ninth round. I suppose I felt very identified with him when I actually saw the pictures of the fight.

significance in regard to sibling rivalry, interfering and being interfered with, but I was not able to pursue it in this session. This was because the patient was now in contact with strong despressive feelings of sympathy for himself and, by extension, with children in general. So I allowed him to go on to finish the session without further attempts at investigation.

I cannot help feeling that the retrospective and introspective account of my experience of working with dreams is a pale thing compared with this "hot" account. But how do they in fact compare in outline? The telling of the dream actually took about five minutes, and while enjoying the vivid narrative I certainly felt completely in the dark at the end of the description. Had I needed to formulate something at that point I could have done no more than relate it to the recent discussion of his "automatic" unfriendly behaviour at school. I felt relieved when the "Moulton" association tied the dream to the previous session, a morning one. It is peculiar that I received such a distinct impression of a reference to the Paris airport when he spoke of "modules", considering that they are, in fact, in their arrangement around the central terminal, called "satellites"; but something about the arrangement of the baskets and the space-age imagery impinged on me quite clearly and was, I feel sure, a correct link. I was on the trail at that point and began to feel excitement permeate the hazy confusion I had experienced while listening to the account of the dream. I was disappointed and not much the wiser when the patient fell silent after the account of the lost suitcases, but the swing to the injured boxer took me by surprise, I felt certain by the end of that association that we were close to something related to his pessimism, but I was still divided in my attention between the "lump of metal" and the "bicycle-like contraption" until the bell rang with the analogy association.

From that moment on the work of formulation began, operating on the background of the mood of pessimism and surprise in the dream. My mind began to weave the material, and the patient joined in the mood of excitement and helped me with his further associations, now not directly stirred by the dream as much as by my beginning to work with it. From the point where I linked the present dream to the six-month old one of the "irate little boy", the patient's mood changed. Had I noticed this earlier I would not have pressed on with my attempts to interpret the dream on the basis of the formulation I had reached. Probably the patient was now so immersed in his identification with the boxer that he paid very little attention to me. Once I realized this, I allowed him to go on with his preoccupation and emotions.

On the whole I would say that this "hot" material matches reasonably well with the general retrospective description. The two together I find fairly convincing as an outline account of the experience of working with dreams, subject to variations.

I promised earlier to spend some time discussing the question of interpretation proper as against formulation of the dream content. This, as I have said, belongs to the larger subject of psycho-analytical method, since it does not in any way bear upon the topic of dream analysis specifically. My own method rests primarily on the investigation of the transference, while reconstruction of the patient's life history is left as a by-product of interest but not, in my opinion, of therapeutic importance. Certainly I hold it as a central tenet of my use of the method that the information, either from patient's recollections or derived from parents or even written records of childhood or infancy, should not be used as evidence for construing the transference. Always the movement should be in the anti-clockwise direction – the construction of the transference should be used for interpreting the meaning of the so-called facts of the history. I regard this re-constructing of the "mythology" of the person's development as a product, and not a root, of the therapeutic impact of the psycho-analytical process.

It will be noticed that in the clinical example of dream analysis the session never really reached a stage of interpretation of the transference. As I was about to launch upon it, from the point of view of the role of sibling rivalry in generating his intolerance to dependence with its resulting tyranny and ingratitude, I noticed that the patient was taken up emotionally in his identification with the injured boxer. This problem, with its outward manifestations in coldness and arrogance of demeanour and apparent unfriend-liness, did in fact become the central issue of the transference for the next two terms. The particular dream I have selected for this chapter, almost at random, became in fact the landmark of a new movement in the transference and was to be referred back to on innumerable occasions.

Nonetheless we may be able to use the material for a brief inves-tigation of the process of interpretation proper, interpretation of the significance of the particular dream. Perhaps it would be use-ful to try to reconstruct what I was about to try to interpret when I noticed that the patient was not really with me, that is, not poised in his attention to me but rather occupied by some strong emotion and its content of identification with the boxer. It would probably have been something like this: "The dream seems to suggest that your relationship with me in the analysis began when I recognized your unfriendly demeanour as a function of timidity in making advances to other people. Almost immediately any sense of gratitude was interfered with by recognition that you were not my only patient but that others had been here before you. Judging from your strong sense of identification with this boxer who, as you said, could hardly put a sentence together, the blow of discov-ering other children must have a reference to the effect upon you in very early childhood, before you could put a sentence together, of the existence of your elder brother. The link to the incident at the Paris airport suggests that this may have coincided with your weaning, the loss of the breast."

It will be seen immediately that this integrated formulation of the transference is not very different from the various interpretive notions that appeared during the phase of wandering about in the material, eliciting associations and generally enriching the ac-count of the dream itself. But it does bring it all into focus in the transference situation whence a reconstructive reference is made. The allusion to babyhood here is presented more for the sake of clarifying the infantile nature of the emotions than for the sake of reconstruction. From the moment that the "analogy" association appeared, this intrepretive formulation began to form in my mind. Twice I attempted to embark upon it but both times the preliminary rounding up of the material met with evidence that the patient was unable to listen because of having gone inside him-self in a depressed state of identification with the boxer.

The point that I would make about my technique of interpretation proper is that it clearly has a rather spiral structure; I seem to circle about in the previous material, linking together the dream elements, the related associations and the interpretive notions until they have all been coralled together. The definitive formulation then comes as a summary of the foregoing. This often takes a few minutes and requires a kind of "holding the floor" against various tendencies in the patient. Usually by this time the patient is eager, even impatient, for the interpretation, but also has a very good idea himself of what is coming. He may want to do it himself, or he may begin to barrack in defiance of it, may "seize the ball and run in the wrong direction", or attempt to forestall the process by a sudden pressure of new material or another dream. In the present case, with this very intelligent and fast-minded youth, I think that he was already there and beyond it, reacting to the depression that the insight was evoking in him.

The question may arise as to the necessity of this step of formalizing the interpretation. I am not convinced that the answer is "yes", even in respect of my own technique. But there is something to be said in the long run for certain dreams which take on a landmark significance for the analysis to be coupled with a formalized interpretation which at least covers the presenting evidence, even though it may be subject to expansion or modification by later material or developments. Where "cover" of the material has notable exceptions (I can detect none in the present material) these probably should be noticed and set aside for clarification by future material.

One comment is worth recording in summary. In this approach to analytical work with dreams, the two phases of dream-exploration and dream-analysis stand apart clearly, both as regards their nature as emotional experiences for analyst and patient, and their role in the work together. Of the two, I feel certain that the exploration is the more important, the more artistic aspect of the work. The patient's growing identification with the analyst's exploratory method is a far more important basis for his gradual development of self-analytic capacity than any striving towards formulation that he may evince.

XI

Dream-Narrative and Dream-Continuity

One of the most impressive evidences of the intrinsic continuity of the process of unconscious phantasy is to be found in the striking links between dreams of the same night or even of successive nights. Attention to this continuity plays a considerable role in the creative use of dream material in analytical work and opens many problems for research, not only in the field of psycho-analysis but in related fields such as linguistics, aesthetics and politics. In speaking of continuity I do not mean to refer to continuity of meaning, but rather continuity of form. Dreams often give an impression, when set out in sequence, of being like an artist's sketches made during the organization of a major composition, or the drawings by children in analysis. It can be seen that a number of central *formal* structures are being drawn up into juxtapositions in order to create a space scintillating with potentiated meaning. Sometimes words and visual forms are seen to interact, as I will shortly demonstrate. At other times spaces are being created as containers of meaning. At other times the movements from one type of space to another, and the emotional difficulties of making such moves, are made apparent.

With this preamble in mind I would like to present a short dream sequence in order to examine the particular question: what increment to our tools of comprehension is gained by viewing dreams as a narrative whose continuity we are able to sample periodically?

The patient is a man in his late thirties, a professional engineer living in a small town some two hours from Oxford and only initially able to come to analysis twice a week pending a change in his life brought about by an estrangement from his wife and the commencement of a new relationship. The upheaval has unbalanced him in various subtle ways, making him willing to accept the advice of his clergyman aimed at salvaging his marriage. This had deteriorated slowly but relentlessly in the years following the birth of his daughter, the second child, and strongly suggested a link to a reputed change in himself as a child subsequent to the birth of his younger sister. The material of the first month of the analysis had strongly suggested a link between his paramour, Beryl, and

148

his sister – perhaps most amusingly in the item of his suddenly falling in love with this young woman, one of a group of mountaineers, while they were eating their lunch on a peak in Wales. He seems to have been rather shy and indolent as a boy, more prone to play with his sister and her friends than to make friends of his own until a period in a new prep school at the age of ten which transformed him into a scholar and athlete of some considerable accomplishment. The repetition of this transformation became clear in the second month of the analysis through exploration of the dream sequence that follows.

In the second week after the Christmas break he brought the following dream: *he was squatting in a rockery with his back to a house overlooking the moors and some yards away six middle-aged women seemed to be looking at him with some disapproval while he absentmindedly fingered an Alpine flower, a "stone-crop", thinking exultantly that he was now divorced, free, no longer a "one-woman guy".* Based largely on previous material (once his helpful but patronizing lecture on Alpine flowers had finished), I suggested that the Christmas holiday had liberated him from the analyst as a possessive and controlling mother (the disapproving women as a collection of part-objects) in favour of an intimate relation to his bottom and anus (the stone-crop) and faeces (the rockery) as, in the past, Beryl was felt to liberate him from his wife, and his sister's birth from his mother. He was a "two-woman guy" and could play them off one against the other. A question about haemorrhoids brought confirmation.

To the following session he brought a dream preceded by the information that he had gone as far as to dig up a "stone-crop" from his garden and place it in a plastic bag to show me before he realized that it was not appropriate to the method I had explained to him at the start of the analysis. He had had a very complicated and peculiar dream: *he was at the church of the village where he had been born but it had been removed stone by stone and erected elsewhere. He was attending Sunday service with Beryl. The minister came romping in dressed in white robes and hood with huge green cat's eyes painted on each side. He arranged the congregation so that the men and women were separated. The patient felt outraged to be kept from Beryl, and left; but to his surprise found himself in the corridor of his grammar school wearing a constricting brown waistcoat that the minister had left for him.* The patient then told me at some length how the change in his life at the age of ten had been wrought by the headmaster, "Whacker" Hill by name, who put fear and admiration into him. A renewal of this experience in the transference seemed strongly suggested. Interpretation of the "stone-crop" dream seemed represented as the "stone-by-stone" transference of the church of his baptism, and also in the "whacking" for playing with his Beryl–sister–bottom which increased the split in his bisexuality (the boys' grammar school and constricting waistcoat).

But far from being galvanized to work by "Whacker Meltzer", he came to the next session in a rather desultory mood and listlessly reported that he had dreamed of being *on the slope below the crest of a Welsh mountain but the scree began to shift and he just let himself be swept over the precipice and was falling to his death unconcernedly.* To the suggestion that this was a representation of rebelling against daddy's authority by falling-in-love with his bottom again, the patient responded with the information about his lunch on the peak and falling in love with Beryl; how different from his slow courtship of his wife. Again he had thought of bringing me a "stone-crop" but had decided not to.

To the Thursday session he brought a fascinating dream which opened up a new vista for exploration, namely the seduction of the daddy-analyst into idealization of his dream-faeces. (Acting-in-the-countertransference may, after all, be a driving force behind some analytic writing). In the dream *he was once again on the slope below the crest of the mountain and again the scree began to slide. But this time he scrambled to a stone out-crop to save himself. When the slide was finished his friend Wilfred edged over and together they peered over the edge to see that the scree had fallen into a perfect geometric shape. The scene then changed and he was romping down the road with two of the secretaries from his office, petting and pummelling each other as one of them carried a plate of food for her old mother.* The patient awakened with an erection. The implication is that he is now a "four-woman guy", that he does not have to fall in love to justify his abandonment of the mother, but can hang on to the breasts. This allows him to be friendly with the daddy who admires his faeces while still managing to romp in private with his nice round bottom while the faeces is being prepared to placate poor old analyst-mummy.

Of course I do not wish to plead the "correctness" of these interpretations; they are only one particular way of viewing the material, bound to a particular framework of phantasy-about-phantasy and a particular poetry for its description. I have selected the material because it seemed to give promise of fruitful exploration with regard to the idea of continuity in dream-life. So let us begin our exploration. For the sake of avoiding confusion, let us start by naming the dreams: a) stone-crop, b) stone-by-stone, c) stone scree, d) stone out-crop.

The first move I wish to make is to investigate the shifting imagery of "stone".

a) There is a rockery in which he is squatting and fingering a flower, a stone-crop. The concept is split into two somewhat idealized portions, the inanimate but decorative rocks, and the animate and tender flower.

b) The stone is again split but now geographically, having been idealized in one place, dismantled and reassembled in another place, thus moving time forward from his baptism to the present.

c) The stone is fragmented into scree and moves, taking him with it into another state of mind, falling, perhaps in love, perhaps to death; it is his state of mind that is also thus either to be passively fragmented or reintegrated by the analysis.

d) The stone is again split into two forms, scree and out-crop, the one endangering, the other saving him; but the fragmented scree is reintegrated as an admired geometrical form.

Now I am in a position to investigate the link between the vicissitudes of 'stone' and of his states of mind in the dream.

a) He is in a triumphant state in relation to the women who disapprove, divorced from his wife and them as the wild moor is divorced from the disciplined rockery.

b) This triumph is undone by the hooded minister who introduces a new divorce, between himself and Beryl (whom we can link with the stone-crop flower) moving him back in time from the present to his grammar-school, mid-way, as it were, between the churches of his baptism and of the present. His mood is finally one of admiring submission, as with "Whacker" Hill.

c) The mood of submission continues, but now it is submission to the movement in space of the fragmented stone, the scree; in abandoning himself to death he falls in love with life, as in the lunch-on-the-peak with Beryl.

d) But once again this idealization (by being divorced from life he finds a new life to fall in love with) is undone by splitting the stone, this time in the form of the scree and the out-crop. Now a move towards a new idealization is set going with the help of friend Wilfred and this sweeps him back to the position in "stone-crop", amplified into promiscuity (one-woman, two-woman and four-woman guy).

How far have we now come? We have raised the possibility that the moods of the dream have a strong correlation with the states of the "stone", but we are uncertain about the meaning and significance of the "stone". Let us see if we can sort this out. My impulse is to link them as follows: rock (of the rockery) – stones (of the

151

church) – stone out-crop, as one series. Series One may be said – from its reference to the church of his baptism, falling in love on the peak and being saved by the outcrop – to represent the concept of the mother's breast. Series Two – judging by the squatting and fingering, the fragmentation and sliding of the scree and the looking down at the geometrical form – to represent his faeces. To this series we can add the tactile qualities of the stone-crop flower, Beryl and the two secretaries. They suggest that his own anus and buttocks serve as the narcissistic alternative to the mother's breast. This is a man who loves mountains, a mountaineer to whom they are both beautiful and dangerous; he is also very proprietary about them and would like to have been a forester rather than an engineer. The "scree" dream suggests that falling to his death and falling in love are perilously linked, while "stone-crop" and "stone out-crop" dreams suggest that being dropped from the breast to his death can be converted through a series of moves thus: fall in love with your own sister-bottom while still clinging to the breast; but this narcissistic union with the Beryl-bottom, while still clinging to the out-crop breast or the new stone-by-stone church, is opposed by the minister-daddy and the new "Whacker" Meltzer-daddy; obviously the thing to do is to seduce the daddy into becoming the Wilfred-friend by showing the geometry of your dream-faeces and the beauty of your stone-crop bottom. On the other hand his history suggests that he was an indolent and effeminate boy until he ran into "Whacker" Hill; the relation with Beryl would be threatened by contamination by this infantile configuration, liable to deteriorate into an impotent playing-with-sister's friends (the secretaries).

The stones of the church and out-crop as objects of his nurture and salvation seemed easily to metamorphose into the stones of the rockery and scree as his faeces, presided over by his idealized anus (stone-crop) and buttocks (Beryl or the two secretaries.) This shift from object dependence to self-idealizing narcissism could be interfered with, however, by the minister-daddy (and "Whacker" Meltzer in the transference). But if his faeces could be idealized in geometric form (dreams) to make an admiring Wilfred-friend of the analyst-daddy, then dependence on the breast and attendant sexual frustration (a one-woman guy) could be obviated in favour of romping promiscuity.

In following this process of shifting back and forth between object-relations and narcissism, we were able to catch a glimpse of other interesting aspects of the patient's relation to time (the new and old churches) and space (up and down, in and out, near and far) as dimensions for the representation by unconscious phantasy of the various levels of development (adult–schoolboy–baby) and corresponding perceptions of his objects and their states of mind and body (the romping minister, the disapproving middle-aged women). The material in toto seems to centre on the question of who is to do the romping at holiday time – the baby-patient or the analyst-parents? Only in his associations about the beneficial effect upon his development of the friendly but firm discipline of "Whacker" Hill-Meltzer do we find evidence of the patient's wish for the analytic experience to continue. We also saw the interesting tendency to put the dream into action by bringing the "stone-crop" specimen to the session, and its actual subtle acting-in-the-transference by bringing such a crop of interesting dreams that the analyst would be rapt in admiration.

Material of this sort seems to illustrate well a continuous problem-solving process going on in the mind of the patient, in the transference, struggling to liberate himself from the tightening bonds of the maternal and paternal transference. At this early stage of the analysis our engineer, despite finding the method fascinating, felt that the analyst, like the clergyman, was bent on returning him to the duties of marriage and fatherhood to repeat what he felt had been the dull and unproductive life pattern of his father. How it comes about that this central word "stone" with its references to flowers, churches, mountains, girlfriends and headmasters, has been selected for the core of the series seems reminiscent of Bion's "selected fact" in its role as crystallizer of thought.

The next clinical example is very different, having far less to do with the oscillation between narcissism and object relations and being more concerned with forming an object of a primal sort that can contain the patient's depression.

An unmarried young man in his third year of analysis had made considerable progress in regard to the confusional states, periods of apathy and psychosexual immaturity which had brought him to treatment, but was finding the week-ends and holidays increasingly daunting as his dependence on the analytic breast slowly replaced his delusional independence based on his intellectual superiority and private wealth. He was producing a whole series of dreams in which the breast was architecturally represented as domes, tents, windmills, etc. On the Wednesday and Friday of one week he produced two such dreams showing his reluctance to abandon his omnipotent intrusiveness into the breast.

On the Wednesday he dreamed that *he was in the ring of a circus tent standing on a slatted structure which suddenly began to spiral up like an escalator carrying him toward an apex and he felt very frightened of falling.*

On the Friday he dreamed that *he was in the street outside a structure such as those used for advertising posters in Paris. It seemed to be the*

153

Communist headquarters and a man was entering with his small son. When the door opened it looked very warm and snug inside and the dreamer realized how cold he was outside.

On the Thursday he had produced a dream whose significance I did not comprehend until the Friday dream had suggested that the dreams of the three days could be arranged together spatially. He had dreamed that *he was in a rectangular room, or rather its two ends bulged inward as a convexity. In the centre was a swimming pool which looked black, he thought, until he noticed that there was no roof and only the night sky was above. The analyst's voice was then heard saying that it might seem lonely at first, but he would quite like it once he was accustomed to it.*

This dream seemed to represent, as a space, the period of waiting with the memory of having been lifted to the breast (the absent object) and the prospect of its repetition – i.e. the linear structure of past–present–future.

It is difficult to say why I found this sequence of dreams so extraordinary. Certainly the Friday dream which closed the "gestalt" took me completely by surprise, and the interpretation was equally unexpected by the patient. It is true that the patient was a painter and writer of some considerable gift and accomplishment, but nonetheless the idea of forming a space in this negative way, a space "implied" rather than constructed, seemed extraordinary and full of aesthetic implications. From the point of view of comprehending how the dream process operates it seemed to illuminate the factor of continuity of forms and their marshalling into juxtapositions of a meaningful sort. It could be said to be genuinely "compositional" in a painterly fashion. But the exciting factor is the way in which the building of the negative form corresponds to its meaning, namely the absence, the space created by the absence of the two objects adjacent to it in time. Somehow the past and the future are made concrete and give this emotive contour to the space of the present. Is it, indeed, a concrete representation of the way in which memory and desire (in Bion's terminology) bind, and we can add, "shape", the experience of the present moment? If, as seems cogently presented, this negative form is a representation of loneliness, it demonstrates the way in which memory of the past and yearning for the future, a future in which the lost object will be recovered, create an emotional space, having the meaning of loneliness, in which no intrinsic qualities for emotional experience can be found except the absence of the qualities of the desired and remembered object. Thus the blackness of the pool is not an intrinsic but a reflected blackness of the night sky, an absence of blueness illuminated by the sun's rays.

As I have said, this second example of continuity in the dream process has a more aesthetic and a less conflictual quality than the "stone-crop" material. It shows a young man, or rather the child in this man, struggling to find a means of representing, and thus of creating, an object which can hold the meaning of his feeling experience in the analytical transference. Its emphasis on formal qualities is clearer than the "stone" which was perhaps the "selected fact" for thought in the previous series. But what they have in common, which may be a major factor in their aesthetic power, is the ambiguity. From the word "stone" there radiates all these lines of associated meaning, at many levels of abstraction. On the other hand the ambiguity of the "pool of loneliness" resides more in its equivocal quality, lacking as it does a positive structure. This space might be the few inches separating the mother's right breast from her left, the fraction of time it takes to shift the baby from one to the other. Or it might be the distance in space, time and sphere of experience between Dante's glimpse of Beatrice and his encounter with her in Paradise. One might wish to compare it with the marvellous space created by a lonely poet:

> Inebriate of air am I
> And debauchee of dew
> Reeling through endless summer days
> From inns of molten blue.
>
> *Emily Dickinson*

XII

Resistance to Dream Analysis
in Patient and Analyst

Although the practice of psycho-analysis in Freud's hands more or less starts with dream analysis as the "highroad to the unconscious", it has had a disappointing history as the decades have slipped past. The literature tells the story clearly, that the painstaking unravelling of dream material through tracing of associations in the manner of the *Traumdeutung*, gave way gradually to an impressionistic mention of them in passing, and finally almost consistent neglect as writers passed on from investigations of psychopathology to polemics on psycho-analytical theory. It has been said by more than one distinguished person that even the teaching of dream-analysis is a matter of historical rather than technical interest.

The renewed interest in dreams which is so characteristic of the Kleinian literature stems clearly from the strong affinity between dream material and the playroom phenomena in work with children – their play, drawings, phantasies, direct transference manifestations. While some of the blame for this neglect can be laid at Freud's door for his more or less pre-psychoanalytic theory about dream mechanics and their trivial place in mental life, the main problem probably resides in the emotional experience of work with dreams. In the previous chapter I have tried to examine the nature of my own method and emotional experience with this aspect of the work, perhaps without fully acknowledging that it has come to play such a central role in my style because I find that it meets some facility, perhaps talent, in me. But while it must be true that patients vary in their talent for remembering dreams, for relating them vividly, perhaps for being able to remember them without progressive distortion, and while it must be similarly true that analysts vary in their talent for envisaging the patient's dream or a near facsimile, probably the more important factors are emotional on both sides – both for and against the full use of this particular tool of our trade.

It does not require a long or extensive experience of supervising students or other analysts to notice that the frequency with which patients present dreams varies directly with the interest, imagination and, by and large, effectiveness with which the analyst receives them. Clearly we are dealing with a problem in the transference-countertransference area. What I have said already almost eliminates the topic of the patient's resistance to dream analysis, but perhaps some comments might be made to round out the subject. Telling a dream is probably the easiest way in which a patient can be truthful with the analyst, largely because he would not know how to distort the material without simply diminishing its meaningfulness. There consequently arises in certain patients, or at certain times with most patients, a resistance to remembering and/or reporting dreams which merely expresses his unwillingness to be open. This would signify either that a delinquent phase, probably with acting out, is in progress, or that a paranoid area has been encountered. Not much needs to be said about either of these aspects of "resistance" to dream analysis for they are general forms of resistance to the work relationship between analyst and patient rather than resistance to any specific insight which is emerging. This, after all, is the central meaning of the concept of resistance in technical theory, resistance against the emergence of an incipient insight. It is perhaps a somewhat archaic concept, belonging to the days of "the solution" of a neurosis and the "working through" of this solution. Whether tacitly or openly acknowledged, few analysts would today think of the transactions in their consulting rooms as fitting this description. In one format or another, a process-view of the transference-countertransference as the main therapeutic agency of analysis has displaced the more active and intellectual approach, and its related demeanour (the "blank screen").

But of course the old terms persevere out of habit without their altered meaning always being recognized or acknowledged. "Resistance" in modern psycho-analysis means, therefore, resistance to deepening emotional involvement in this transference-countertransference process. Bion puts the case pithily when he says that most patients do not have to offer resistance, they know how to mobilize the analyst's resistance to deeper participation. In both partners in the work, resistance is therefore not mobilized against emerging insight but constitutes a varying attitude towards psychic reality, the acknowledgement of internal world figures and transactions. Much of this has been traced already in the chapters on the borderlands between dreams and actions, dreams and hallucinations. But a word needs to be said about the sad plight of the patient who is eager for analysis to break through this denial of psychic reality which keeps him in a state of impoverished imagination and emotionality but cannot, despite all efforts, manage to remember dreams.

157

I do not wish to direct attention to patients whose acting in the transference is so copious that, like small children, their dreams are directly transformed into behaviour in the consulting room. There is another class of patient, often coming to analysis for professional reasons, either primarily or at least ostensibly, whose intellectual knowledge, devotion to psycho-analysis and readiness for sacrifice to enjoy its benefits would seem to make them ideally suited to this method. But after a few weeks or months and a few experiences of dream analysis, their dream-life simply disappears from view. They have the continually tantalizing awareness of having dreamed, of having remembered dreams on awakening in the night, even of having written them down, but no live memory of the experience can be recaptured in the full light of day. It is a type of deprivation from which they suffer. Is it a kind of dream-anorexia? No, they hunger for the dream. Is it carelessness? Are they robbed of their dreams? Do the dreams seem constructed of stuff with too short a half-life to persevere in memory for more than a few minutes.?

In my experience this sad process (which does not necessarily interfere with analytic progress since plenty of other evidence for construing the transference makes its appearance in anecdote, memory, acting out and phantasy) can usually be traced to an important aspect of the organization of the patients' narcissism. One discovers that in their way of life a great deal of delegation of responsibility takes place. It is not that they avoid the responsibility of thinking or making decisions. On the contrary, they are often people with a great capacity in this regard and even a talent for organization and administration. But they seem to be great delegators of action, prone to mobilize lieutenants to perform what amounts to the "dirty work". If dreams could be reported by the equivalent of using a credit card instead of having to carry money about, the analysis would be full of them. So it seems to correspond a bit with the patient who loses his bill, is always late in paying. He is not mean or begrudging – if only he could pay by standing order.

With these cursory remarks I wish to turn to the main substance of this chapter which bears not only on the practice of dream analysis by the individual analyst, but also on the general place of dream-analysis in our training programmes, literature, congress panels, and in collateral fields of applied psycho-analysis. My general thesis is this: contrary to the dictates of common sense, which say that the analyst's resistance to deeper involvement in the transference-countertransference is mobilized by the impact of acting-in-the-transference by the patient (or fears of the consequences of his acting-out), closer scrutiny suggests that it is the intense intimacy of dream-analysis which is the driving factor. It will be ar-

gued that dream analysis can be conducted with the ideal of absti-
nence that Freud so strongly advised and is a great bulwark against
the dread of being drawn into acting-in-the-counter-transference.
This may be true of the inexperienced analyst, or of the student
who has been assailed by horror stories and cautionary tales about
sexual behaviour. But for the experienced analyst the great occu-
pational hazard of this work lies in the exposure to radioactive
material – to use an analogy.

No material that a patient brings to his analyst is as powerfully
evocative as his dream material. Naturally so, for it stems directly
from the most creative and passionate levels of his mental functioning. All but the most powerful evocations of literary and
graphic art (I will not include music here, mainly from ignorance)
pale in comparison with dream-material for ability to stick in the
mind. It is no surprise that of the torrents of anecdote, phantasy
and behaviour with which he is assailed in his working day, what
stays most vividly in the analyst's memory, and therefore is most
prominent in his notes, is the dream material. And while an analyst
may easily forget the facts of his patient's life, his father's profession, the number of his siblings or children, his educational history
– despite having heard them innumerable times – he is unlikely
completely to forget his patient's dream unless his resistance has
prevented him from analysing it. Correspondingly he may confuse one patient's anecdotal or historical material with that from
another patient, but he will hardly ever mistake the owner of a
dream that he has remembered from an earlier session.

The nature of the anxieties aroused in the analyst by the strong
evocative impact of dream material can easily be divided into
categories such as fear of invasion, dread of confusion, intolerance
of impotence.

I will assume in the following discussion that the analyst in question has both a theoretical respect for dream-analysis as part of his
technical equipment, and has developed sufficient skill in the investigation and elucidation of dreams so that failure to understand
a particular dream or sequence of dreams impinges upon him as
a particular phenomenon in his countertransference.

Fear of invasion

For analysts, since they have become accustomed through their
own analysis and through work with patients to hearing and recit-
ing dreams, hearing another person's dream is an experience of
intimacy about which they have perhaps become blasé. They have
forgotten that it is a most unusual event in daily life for one person
to recite a dream to another, particularly if it is a recent dream,

and especially if the listener also appeared in the manifest content. Therefore they have also forgotten the embarrassment that this extraordinary intimacy excites as well as the feeling of invasion that accompanies it. I think it is true that there is no more vivid way of communicating a state of mind than by telling a dream, but by virtue of its vividness the dream image thus conveyed also has little fish hooks from which the listening mind may find itself unable very easily to shake free. In this sense it is like the impact of pornography. Because the dream of a patient tends to remain more vividly in the analyst's mind than any anecdotal material, it is subject to the same tendency within the analyst's mind as it has in the patient's, namely the tendency to be acted out. This of course touches on the relationship of dreams not only to pornography but to art. But the evocative power of the patient's dream is more likely to fall into the latter than the former category by reason of the operation of anxiety under which it was produced. This is not by any means true of all dreams in analysis; there are certainly dreams of resolution of conflict which have a powerful aesthetic impact, but they are of course in the minority.

In other words, fear of invasion by the patient's projective identification of a disturbed part of his personality can play a paralysing role in the analyst's approach to the investigation of a dream. He may find that he has forgotten the manifest content by the time the patient has told him some associations; or conversely, that the projected image is so powerful that he is unable to direct his attention to the associations.

Dread of confusion

I do not mean to discuss here the times when the patient is using the format of dream-reporting for the specific purpose of generating confusion in the analyst's mind. The technique for doing this is fairly easily recognized; dream content and associations are so interwoven that the resulting patchwork of dream and reality must be painstakingly teased apart. I wish to refer to dreams in which the patient's states of confusion are so subtly represented that the analyst is no more able to make the requisite differentiations than is the patient. This particularly refers to confusion between good and bad figures, and therefore between parts of the self and parental objects; also confusions of geography and zones (see my *Psycho-analytical Process*, 1967, Heinemann, London.) In such a situation the analyst may find that his mind veers off from the dream and follows only the associations, eventually even seeming to ignore the fact that a dream has been presented. His problem may be found in his failure to utilize the countertransference fully in comprehending the dream. It is usually the emotionality inhabiting the dream which gives the surest clues to these differentiations, especially where ethical values are concerned. Too prompt a use of the rational faculty for making differentiations tends to leave the analyst in the lurch, much as the patient is prone to be swayed in his own ethical judgments where these are founded on argument rather than on emotion. It is necessary for the analyst, when he finds himself confused by the dream, to wait for his emotional intuition to become firmly established; then he can retrace the evidence of dream and associations to document his intuition. He is liable otherwise to be in the state equivalent to the "hung jury" for whom the evidence is contradictory because one of the witnesses is lying.

Intolerance of impotence

One of the pitfalls of the analytical use of dreams is the expectation of the so-called "mutative interpretation" (Strachey); the analyst's therapeutic zeal tends to take the form of expecting that the marshalling of evidence will "convince" the patient, much in the spirit of Freud's early work before the paper on "working through". Habitual disregard by the patient of the evidential value of dreams can greatly dampen the analyst's interest in working with them. The patient's persistent attitude that "it is only a dream" is, after all, not without its historic status; Freud himself viewed dreams as of little significance other than as a patchwork of day-residues and distortions having the trivial aim of enabling the sleeper to sleep on undisturbed. Patients with a strong tendency to deny psychic reality intuitively agree with this posture and manifest their contempt for the dream and for the analyst's use of dreams. They behave as if the analyst were trying them for some mythical crime in relation to which they stand protected by Habeas Corpus.

But analysts may also share this attitude unconsciously even when it is foreign to their theoretical framework of reference. The trouble is often found to lie in the problem of their attitude towards psycho-analytical responsibility. The spectre of lawsuits, coroner's courts and irate relatives may weigh heavily upon them in the course of analytical work. They have difficulty in accepting the fundamental impotence of the analyst *vis à vis* the patient's psychic structures. They find the responsibilities incommensurate with the powers to implement their judgments. But after all, this is the dilemma of parents as well – not so clear in early childhood but shockingly apparent with their adolescent children.

Therefore the patient who denies psychic reality may often not manifest it by failure to remember nor by failure to report his dreams, but rather through his attitude towards the procedure as a foible of the analyst, generative perhaps of information for the analyst but devoid of evidential significance for the patient. If the analyst allows himself to be intimidated by such a cavalier attitude he may easily relinquish the use of this powerful method – powerful, that is, for penetrating the meaning of unconscious events even though it is powerless to convince. Freud himself, in the long run, as "Analysis Terminable and Interminable" testifies, was discouraged by this aspect of analytical work. While the dictum about "leading a horse to water" may seem identical with Freud's conclusion that in the final tally it is the economics of the mind that dictate the outcome, there is a great difference on close examination. When the analytical method is viewed as a process having its origins and format within the patient, only presided over and facilitated by the analyst, his tolerance of the impotence of his position with the patient is likely to be greatly strengthened.

In drawing this brief investigation to a close, it seems necessary to mention an aspect of analytical work with patients' dreams which, while implied in what has gone before, needs perhaps to be stated unequivocally. In my experience the emotional situation between analyst and patient at the non-transference level (as two adult people working together at a task with knowledge, skill and an agreed format of procedure) at no point reaches such heights of pleasure, intimacy and mutual confidence as in the unique process of dream-analysis. The reason for this is to be found in the aesthetic level of experience in both participants which abandonment to the "poetic diction" of dreams facilitates; it brings out artistic creativity in both partners and produces an oeuvre, the dream and its interpretation, which both members can experience as generated by combined creativity.

XIII

The Relation of Dreaming to Learning from Experience in Patient and Analyst

In analysis we usually study dreams to gain access to processes of thinking that concern the patient's emotional conflicts. But every once in a while, particularly with patients who are students of analysis or are professionally interested in the analytic method itself, a different sort of dream arises. These are dreams that seem to reflect the patient's thinking about how his mind works. They are what might be called "theoretical" dreams; they are not about psycho-analysis proper but the patient's own theory about his experience of his mind's operation.

Throughout the history of psycho-analysis, the so-called "theories of the mind" have been the changing models of the mental apparatus that analysts think they are using in listening to, observing and trying to understand their patients and themselves. Freud's own models changed during the course of his work. The first model postulated by him resembled some kind of telephone exchange and this he elaborated, before he started on his psychoanalytic work, in what is known as "The Project for a Scientific Psychology". This was a neurologist's model and was concerned with the apparatus that conducts messages in the brain; it had nothing to do with the meaning of the messages but only with the way in which the messages were distributed and conducted through the neural network. Once he embarked upon analytic work he elaborated a second theory which was, in a way, a supplement to the first, namely the Libido theory. This was a theory about the distribution of "mental energy" in which mental energy and sexual excitation were more or less equated with one another. But then, in the course of his work, he discovered that the central problem was conflict which had various configurations; conflict between what he called the Ego and the outside world; conflict between the Ego and the Super Ego; and between the Ego and the instincts. So he elaborated the Structural theory (in the 1920's) in which he spoke of the Ego as serving three masters. This envisaged the mind as an apparatus for conciliation whose central function was to reconcile the demands coming from these three directions

– a negotiating instrument. It seemed natural, from the employ-
ment of that model, that this central part of the mind, the Ego,
should then be viewed as being mainly concerned with maintain-
ing peace of mind (the Nirvana principle). None of the models he
devised took any serious account of emotionality and its meaning
– this was left for Melanie Klein to develop in her theory of the
internal world. This was a great advance since it envisaged the
mind as a kind of internal theatre with figures entering into emotional relationships and conflicts with one another, from which
meaning was generated and deployed into the external world and
external relationships. What the theory lacked was any interest in,
or concern with, the thinking processes themselves; it seemed to
take for granted that the mind was able to think, to perform thinking functions, as if that were not a problem for psycho-analytical
investigation but could be left to the philosophers and academic
psychologists.

This theory was at a similar stage of scientific development as
Embryology had been before the development of Genetics. It was
purely descriptive of the way the mind elaborates its particular
phantasies and pictures of the world, and quite unconcerned with
the means used to do this. It remained for Bion to consider this
particular psychological problem further and to elaborate his
Theory of Thinking which we are now beginning to explore.

Reading psycho-analytical literature gives one the impression
that analysts operate in their consulting rooms using certain
theories and that they make their interpretations accordingly. But
it is important to remember that papers are not written in the
course of analytic sessions; they are written in retrospect and they
are written to be read by colleagues. They must be stated in some
previously agreed language. Hence they are statements that imply
the following kind of preamble: "If we accept that we are operating according to pre-existing theories, then what happens in my
consulting room could be stated in this particular way." However,
what in fact happens in the consulting room is basically no different from what happens in any science, which is this: we have an
instrument, whose structure is analogous to the object that it is
trying to study, which registers certain responses to that object, its
behaviour or its structure. This holds whether we are talking about
an electrical instrument for studying the inside of the cyclotron,
or a photographic instrument used for photographing the sections of a cell, or any other instrument. But whatever the instrument of study, it has to have a structure analogous to the object
under study in order that it can make responses that have some
intelligible relationship to what is being studied. And from that
point of view psycho-analysis is the perfect science because it

164

employs an instrument not just analogous to the object but nearly identical with it. Using its harmonic response of countertransference, we study clinical phenomena.

For this reason any paper in the field of scientific psychoanalysis that is an honest report of clinical experiences is fundamentally introspective and autobiographical. Therefore, in a sense, it aspires to being a work of art. Psycho-analytic research is essentially self-scrutiny and self-description, its primary instrument being introspection. It has, therefore, a strong link with the philosophical method and can be said to take up a very comfortable methodological position in the triangle created traditionally by science, philosophy and the arts.

Psycho-analytical papers, I suggest, can also be seen as technical papers about the psycho-analytic method and how the analyst's mind seems to operate in the analytic situation. This is very similar to what happens in the arts where painters are always exploring paint as a method of representing their life experiences; musicians explore the use of sound with the same idea, and literary artists likewise are attempting the same exploration of words. A close link therefore exists between the psycho-analytic method as a research into technique, and the arts as research in craftsmanship.

As an extension of this thought I return to those dreams which I mentioned at the beginning. They are presented rarely by particularly introspective people who are interested in the psycho-analytic method; they are dreams that seem to be an exploration of problems of thinking.

The two dreams we are about to consider came after three years of analysis which had brought about significant changes in the patient's character as well as leading to her changing her professional emphasis from administration to research in her field. These dreams occurred when she was studying Bion's work on groups and his Theory of Thinking.

In the first dream *there was a table to be set for dinner, with maybe some six to eight places. The patient had been delegated to set out the cutlery which was all mixed up together in a drawer. It seemed a perfectly simple task. However, when she started the whole situation continually escalated in complexity; the table grew bigger, the number of places more numerous, and the variety of the different types of cutlery kept increasing and increasing; there were silver, wooden and artistic implements – knives for sculpture and modelling, pencils and pens, brushes and rulers. So she decided that she would have to change her method. She would try to accomplish the task in the same way that one would collate papers that have been duplicated, say 50 pages and 100 copies; she would organize the implements and deal them out systematically. Pretty soon it became clear that this method too was not going to be adequate to cope with the escalation, and that some*

165

other method was needed – a machine of some sort would have to be devised. She ended up by feeling that she was confronted by an impossible task, like Hercules in the Augean stables. There would have to be some sort of extremely complicated apparatus that would be able to cope both with the growing complexity as well as with the ever escalating volume of work.

The second dream was very different. In this *she had three simple tasks to perform, and she had been given a simple instrument with which to work – a thread. First, she had to repair one of the links in a gold chain which had been given to her by her mother* (and which, in fact, she had lost just a week before). *The thread was to be used to tie the links together so that the chain could be worn. Second, there was a necklace of little polished stones* (this she had bought in an open market on a trip made some years ago). *The necklace's thread had stretched so that it was necessary to restring the beads. Here she was concerned about whether she would be able to make the little knots that separated each bead and which held them securely so that they did not all fall off if the thread broke. Third, there was a dress in which one of the seams had become unstitched and this had to be repaired.*

This third item had a certain background in the analysis during its third month when I had told her of a six inch split in her trouser seam because I knew that she was going to a meeting and would be very embarrassed if she discovered it later.

These two dreams came, then, at a time when the patient was studying Bion's work. She was more particularly studying the Grid and trying to understand what alpha-function could be. It therefore seems a reasonable hypothesis that the first dream represents a way of trying to imagine what alpha-function accomplishes, while the second dream is a reference to the Grid and the kind of mental functions which the Self can perform as they are implied in the different categories of the Grid. In other words the two dreams distinguish between unconscious mental functions performed by internal objects (the breast at infantile level), and mental functions (conscious or unconscious) which lie within the capacity of parts of the Self.

Let us go back to the first dream and consider the initial situation of setting a table for six or eight people. In group psychological terms it is possible to think about people and to classify them, as in the army for instance, according to a few simple determinants – Name, Rank and Serial Number. It might be argued that this is a perfectly adequate classification and that it could be managed by the conscious mind. However, as soon as we begin to describe people as individuals rather than merely name them as members of a class, we become aware of a continually escalating complexity revealed by the on-going experience of each individual's mind and person. We soon realize that it is impossible to think about them and reach any understanding of them as individuals with our conscious mind – we have to abandon ourselves to some other apparatus over which we have no control. This is a tenable context within which the first dream could be placed.

On the other hand the second dream seems to be an investigation into what a person *can* do with his conscious mind, the sort of useful functions that can be controlled. It gives three examples – the gold chain, the bead necklace, and the repair to the dress. First, to put it in the context of Bion's work, each of the three different tasks in the second dream undertakes the repair of damage that has been done by "attacks on linking". (The link has been broken, stretched or disengaged.) It is also interesting to notice that the three kinds of links are all different: the gold chain is composed of links that are joined by interlocking one with another; the beads are all arranged on a single thread, but each item is separated and kept in place by a knot (which I think is also a pun meaning "a is not b, is not c, is not d" and so on, but the beads are also held firmly together by something that they all have in common); the two pieces of material are held together, like her trousers, by a thread that joins them, but it joins them in such a way that they make a shape, and the whole thing becomes three-dimensional.

In a way, of course, the second dream is much more interesting than the first which does not get any further than does Bion when he says "alpha-function" – by which he would seem to mean something that we do not understand anything about, something perhaps essentially mysterious and probably immensely complicated. However, this representation is of particular importance to this patient who has moved from preoccupation with group processes to studying the complexity of individual intimate relationships. To that extent it is characteristic of a whole series of dreams which occupied her analysis at this point. All represented in one form or another the need and fear of abandoning control and surrendering herself to emotional experience; this was sometimes represented as floating down a river, sometimes as being carried in a vehicle whose destination she did not know.

In the second dream there is the important problem of preserving and repairing what she has received from the mother, the analyst and other people. It is clearly suggested that if a link gets broken, and you do not notice it in time, you may lose the object and never be able to recover it. Whether this is true of the mental apparatus I am not sure, but it is certainly the nature of the anxiety which the dream is attempting to resolve. One might say: "If you notice the damage in time, you do have the means of repairing it with your own little thread of thinking, which may not produce gold links but it does prevent loss of the object."

Both dreams also relate to another of Bion's concepts: distinction between symbiotic and commensal relationships. We see here a representation of people being at the same table – the commensal relationship. From that point of view it can be seen that the symbolic structure of the two dreams is very similar – the places arranged around the table and the chain of gold links or necklace of beads around the neck. While the precious chain from mother is structured by linking, the necklace of common beads is held together by a common thread of separating knots. Compare this with the representation of individuals seated round the table, having something in common (commensal) – or will it be discovered when the utensils are all sorted, that each is intimately linked to its neighbour on the right and on the left (symbiotic)?

Returning to the second dream, I find that the open seam in the dress is particularly interesting because it might be seen to represent being able to make a conceptual garment that really does fit a person – you know that it is not the actual person himself; it is only a conception that you have fitted onto the person. But you have to be able to make it so that it both fits and does not fall to pieces. There is also a link with the story of the Emperor's New Clothes.

It might be said then, that the first two examples (the gold chain and the beads) have to do with the problem of understanding people's relationships to one another, how they are linked together, how they are separated, how they are similar and how they are different; but the third example, that of the seam in the dress, reflects a much more complicated approach to the individual in his own right. Thus the dream seems to be seeking an integration of the patient's former socio-political interests and her newer more psycho-analytical ones.

The first dream could also have a bearing on overcoming the delusion of independence, not only from an internal object but from objects in the external world as well. If we list the equipment that we use in our daily life, from our getting up to our going to bed again, it would include the whole technological equipment of our culture. Where does a concept of independence stand in that context? Where is the "self-made man"? What does "think for oneself" mean?

We have before us, then, a beautiful example of a person struggling to learn from experience; experience of her analysis, her reading and experience of life in general. She has taken Bion's poetry (alpha-function, the Grid, attacks on linking, commensal and symbiotic relationships) and found her own symbolic representations in the forms of everyday life. She has woven them together with her appreciation of the beauty and value of the analytical experience, on to the background of her infantile appreciation of her mother. It forms a dream tapestry of surprising superficial simplicity and of deep complexity. Nothing that has been said so far is in the nature of psycho-analytical interpretation of the dream, merely a "reading" of its manifest content and implications, knowing its background in her studious preoccupations. It adds nothing to the meaning of the dream but is, rather, a pale paraphrase. The dream image will remain in the mind of patient and analyst long after my prose translation of it has faded. It has "poetic diction" indeed, with the simplicity of a Vermeer.

It can be said with confidence that by this dream operation an intelligent and sensitive young woman is making these ideas "her own" in the sense that Bion means by "becoming O". Furthermore by communicating her dream to me the patient has helped me to think of these matters with a greater clarity than I had ever managed before. I had certainly never seen so clearly the differential nature of the commensal and symbiotic link as the one implied here by the distinction between the gold-linked chain and the string of beads or the people seated around the table, either symbiotically linked by varied but overlapping equipment, or commensally linked to one another by identical implements.

XIV

Recovery from Analysis and the Self-analytic Method

The dictum that the patient's neurosis is converted into a trans-ference neurosis of which the analysis endeavours to cure him, may be an oversimplification but it has more than a grain of truth in it. In so far as the analysis enables the patient to gather together into a single relationship the diverse threads of his infantile trans-ference tendencies, it can be seen to make a concentration of infan-tile need, anxiety and affect which has every resemblance to an illness. Where this replaces processes of symptom formation that were hampering the patient's activities and relationships in the outside world, it may appear as a benefit to the disinterested ob-server. But where the emotional disorder in the personality has been bound in character or in patterns of relationship, the con-centration and potentiation of the transference processes made possible by the psycho-analytical setting may show as an illness in a person previously considered well and well-adjusted by family and friends. This is perhaps most often seen in people who come to analysis not from motives of therapy, but for professional reasons of one sort or another.

Fifteen years ago (*The Psycho-analytical Process*, Heinemann, London, 1967) I suggested the usefulness of viewing psycho-analytical treatment from a process point of view, that is of a con-tinuum of transference-countertransference events which the analyst monitored, contained in his setting, and tried to assist with interpretation. In this view the content of the process was seen to emerge from the unconscious of the patient as an externalization of his internal object relations and narcissistic organization, while the analyst was described as "presiding" over its evolution. It was a view that had become borne in upon me mainly through work with children but which had proved equally applicable to the situ-ation with adult patients.

Since that time my explorations of technique have been closely related to this process view and in some papers I have tried to extend or clarify its implications and findings. Perhaps chief amongst these implications was an altered view of the analyst's role *vis à vis* the goals or aims of therapy; namely, that he was totally relieved of any such responsibility. This in turn had implications for the concept of the "completed" analysis and the decision for termination. In the "Process" view, the "natural history" of the transference included a weaning process which the analyst needed only to recognize and respect. But this often seemed to place the therapist, as well as the patient, in some conflict in relation to their individual, or sometimes shared, hopes and expectations, even where these were not framed or erected as goals. It was noticeable in my own work, as well as in that of people I supervised, that the outcome of the analysis, however satisfactory from the "Process" point of view, was felt as deeply disappointing from the descriptive vertex. Symptoms might have gone, external circumstances might have improved – often the patient would have to admit that every reasonable requirement for happiness was now at hand – but the patient still felt ill, perhaps in an indefinable way. The consequence was a deep reluctance to finish, and a focus of distrust that stood painfully in conflict with better feelings towards the analyst. I noticed that I too often felt troubled, uncertain, worried, inclined to procrastinate. This was particulary true when the weaning process set in earlier than usual, according to my training and prior experience, after two and a half or three years in some cases, or under the pressure of external events such as a pregnancy or a job opportunity abroad.

For some years the situation impinged upon me paradoxically. On the one hand I felt a growing conviction about the beauty and goodness of the psycho-analytical method, a growing confidence in my own way of working and a correspondingly increased misgiving about the value to the patients of the process they had experienced. We could see and agree that their lives were changed, but whether it was a change for the better seemed open to grave doubt. I consequently began to be a bit more insistent, though this was hardly ever necessary, about establishing a more formalized follow-up period with occasional letters reporting circumstances and a sample of dreams and self-analytic work, punctuated by rare consultations. To my surprise the patients always, in the rare consultations of the first two years, lay on the couch and carried on an analytic session, although this had not been my intention. The content of letters and sessions was strikingly patterned, beginning with optimistic reports of work or family life, followed gradually by deepening gloom about inner states of unhappiness, symptoms, loneliness and isolation, and ending in an attempt to reassure me while hinting that a resumption of analysis should perhaps be considered.

These three categories of behaviour and attitude varied from individual to individual and from time to time, but the pattern was fairly fixed. In the face of this I decided to place my greatest reliance on dream material and the evidence of self-analytical capacity. By this means I was able to resist even the occasional clamorous demand for resumption of treatment, including threats to go to another analyst (which one patient did, in fact, do for a time). In all of this, and perhaps the most sustaining to me in my uncertainty, was the evidence of a considerable gulf between warm personal feelings and disturbed infantile trust, with its corresponding countertransference.

During this time, having a wide supervision practice, I had the comforting experience of seeing that the phenomena described above were not idiosyncratic to my style of work. It could also be seen with impressive uniformity in the cases of my colleagues who had for some time been utilizing a "Process" point of view in their consulting rooms. And as my hopefulness returned it was accompanied by a new realization, that a time eventually came which marked a turning point in the post-analytic period. The behaviour of my former analysands would change and take on one of two forms. Either the patient drifted away or else he made a move to establish a non-analytical type of relationship. The drifting took the form of more cursory letters, fewer and farther between, with less information and an absence of complaints, while the consultations became face to face interviews and then ceased. My impression was very distinct: I was no longer an important person in the ex-analysand's life; a cooler assessment of me as a person had taken place with the result that the high estimate of my personal value, attractiveness, ethical standards and position in the world had waned, not without disappointment, and apparently without very specific grounds for disillusionment. The radiance of the transference and the halo effect of its mist had disappeared; the impact on me was mixed pain and reassurance.

Where a non-analytical relationship was sought, the advances were shy and tentative, mainly along professional lines, gradually implementing a transition from the formality of the analytical setting. My impression is that the determinants of this behaviour lay largely with the patients, judging by the fact that the degree of movement towards social or professional friendship seemed often to have a poor correlation with my own degree of affection for the person. Or perhaps it was a bit paradoxical that where my affection was the greatest, the former patients found it most necessary to keep their distance – for a time at least.

It was during this second period, which seldom ensued in less than two years, that the patient began to feel well and I began to feel confident that the analysis had done some good. The realization came as a surprise to me and altered my view of my own analy-

tical experiences as a patient, the first of which had been inter-
rupted by military service and the second by the death of my
analyst during the termination process. I remember that when I
returned from service to see my first analyst to tell him that I was
going abroad to complete my training, I could hardly speak but
wept for half an hour and had to leave. I had assumed this to be a
manifestation of guilt for my treachery until we met socially some
years later and he helped me to see it differently. I had also assumed that the acute misery, feeling of dying and loneliness after
Melanie Klein's death were peculiar to the circumstances rather
than to the process. But I have come to think differently about this
too as I have watched patient after patient re-experience the suffering of the baby during weaning.

It does not seem likely that specific clinical material would
greatly add to the clarity of this description of the phenomena.
Also, the question of discretion seems particularly delicate in this
area. So I will go on to investigate and discuss the problems thrown
up by these observations.

From the "Process" point of view the psycho-analytical method,
following Bion's formulation, can be viewed as a special instance
of group activity, a two-member group gathered for the purpose
of studying the patient's experience of the world as an individual.
This corpus of experience will be seen to stand in apposition to a
second body of transactions, namely his involvements in larger
human groups as a member, functioning either on the basis of
group mentality (valency, proto-mental phenomena, etc.) or sci-
entifically (learning from experience, aimed at development,
bound to reality, both internal and external). In the two-member
group three different types of events can be discerned to form an
organization in time, one being the work-group collaboration with
the analyst, the second a narcissistic "ganging" with or against the
analyst, and the third bound to basic assumptions of pairing, dependence or fight-flight, and characterized by mindless slogan
and cliché in a very primitive transference-countertransference.

Within this three-fold organization of relationships in the
analytical setting two distinct forms of movement can be discerned. One of these is a movement to and fro from individuality
to group mentality; the other is a movement to and fro from object
relationship to narcissistic organization. The two areas are
bridged at the level of narcissistic organization which allows for
easy transition from individual to group mentality. (It will be
noticed that this way of viewing the analytical situation begins to
have a certain resemblance to the approach of Levi-Strauss to
sociological problems.)

If the analytical situation and process are viewed on this model,

173

the initial gathering into the analytical setting of the infantile transference processes extant in the patient's life will naturally be accompanied by a clarification of his relationships outside the analysis, due to a lessening of confusion of the levels operative there. This in turn will be punctuated by periodic aggravation during analytical breaks or at times of eruption of acting out. But despite this clarification, which usually results in increased effectiveness and pleasure in relations and work, along with a lessening of symptoms, the patient will on the whole feel more ill. His conception of himself as an ill person will have become more pointed and intense because the gathering in of his infantile transference tendencies will have brought these previously scattered processes into greater proximity to one another and will have confronted them with a setting in which collusion between the unconscious phantasies and corresponding defences against mental pain will be minimized by the method (and personality) of the analyst.

This is merely another way of describing the transference neurosis (Freud) and transference psychosis (Rosenfeld). The analyst's task in presiding over the setting and in attempting to modulate and even modify anxieties by interpretation is, in the first instance, to preserve this gathering together of the infantile transference processes. In order to do this the setting must be sufficiently successful in this modulation (when coupled with the cooperation of the patient through insight into the method) to compete with the opportunities abounding in the patient's life outside the analysis. These opportunities include other forms of treatment, other transference-countertransference relationships (particularly with the original parents, spouse and children), other systems of thought (religions, political parties, economic structures), methods of ablating mentality (drugs, sex, hobbies, making money, etc.).

But the immediate fruit of successful modulation of the patient's mental pain is, as I have said, a deepening conviction of being an ill person. This may in fact be accompanied by a lessened feeling of inferiority to others on the score of illness, but this ceases to be any comfort as consideration of psychic reality moves to a more prominent position in the patient's value systems. At the same time that psychic reality becomes more important, there grows in the patient an awareness of the complexity of the mind and a corresponding feeling of despair at its possible infinitude, mystery, impenetrability. He can neither see where the analysis is heading nor can he muster the spirit of adventure sufficient to enjoy the uncertainty. The conviction grows upon him that if he had know at the beginning that it would be so different from his expectations he would never have embarked upon it. Now he is like a passenger at sea; he can neither jump overboard nor feel confidence in the captain who talks vaguely and wildly about sailing westwards to India.

But as the analysis continues, as confusional states begin to resolve, problems of dependence and the oedipal conflict take the centre of the analytical stage, love begins to dawn in the misty morning of infantile dependence. The patient's illness begins to reveal itself to him as a transference illness. He now comes to the sessions in pain and leaves happy over and over again, and the happiness of *feeling* (not necessarily *being*) understood and known to the depths seems a greater happiness than he has ever known and superior in quality to the happiness of his other relationships outside the analysis. Yet it must end: "We can't go on meeting like this", as the joke puts it. Like the other joke of transforming the untreatable common cold into the treatable pneumonia, the analysis seems to have cured the patient's persecutory illness by making him love-sick, but he does not believe this is treatable except by living-happily-ever-after in some form of intimacy, preferably sexual, with the analyst or his countersexual representative outside the analysis.

The position of the patient is not far distant from the state of mind of the analyst, who may know from his experience that internalization of the relationship is possible and is in reality the only basis for true independence. But he cannot feel any confidence that it will be managed by the patient or be wholeheartedly encouraged or allowed by himself. This is especially so where parental love in the countertransference is compounded by growing affection in the collaborative relationship (W-group, working alliance, adult level of relationship, etc.).

It is against this background that patient and analyst are called upon to make an act of relinquishment, a leap-in-the-dark (to borrow Kierkegaard's phrase) which is the prerequisite for the operation of the process of internalization in all its mystery. If either or both hesitate and delay, a process equivalent to the anaemia of the infant-too-long-on-the-breast sets in, the transference-countertransference love is soured by guilt towards the "next baby" who is being kept waiting and termination-by-exhaustion may ensue. In order to be able to make this leap himself and to inspire enough trust for the patient to accept it well, the analyst must be convinced that the transference is an emanation of psychic reality in the first instance and that the so-called "internalization by introjection" is an illusion induced by the patient's reluctance to contain, and therefore be responsible for the preservation of, anything precious. In fact the transference is not really "introjected"; its internal origin in the reality of internal objects is reluctantly *discovered*.

Some ten years ago, when these ideas became quite firm, a strange experience began to form part of my professional practice. It usually started with supervision of colleagues, some older, some younger than myself, but would suddenly turn into a request for re-analysis. Sometimes the previous analyst was ill or deceased, sometimes the professional relationship had become too close for resumption of analysis to be considered. The requests seldom involved any grievance towards previous analyst(s). On the contrary – gratitude played some part in the reluctance to trouble that person further.

These requests bore a striking similarity to the times when my own patients, in follow-up, had suggested further analytic work, and the satisfactory outcome of resistence to these requests strengthened me to resist those coming from other sources. Instead I suggested an attempt to work out a method of supervising the person's self-analysis of their dream life. In fact it was often the case that any systematic or even enthusiastic sporadic work of that sort had ceased years earlier, but it was easily revived. The method that was arranged and accepted was based absolutely on the supervision relationship which I tend to carry on very informally, sometimes with coffee, avoiding completely any commentary on transference or countertransference phenomena. Responsibility for managing emotions and impulses at that level were explicitly agreed to be tacitly handled by each individual privately. The feasibility of the method is entirely dependent on both being able to do this, to operate as a two-person work group.

Meeting weekly or fortnightly has to be adhered to except in an emergency, which in fact hardly ever happens. In all respects the method involves a supervision of the person's relationship to himself as patient. In time, persons known to me only socially and others who were institutional associates but with whom I had had no previous contact, also appeared asking for re-analysis, but willing to try this less costly method. Over the past twelve years I have used this method with mutual interest, pleasure and, it would seem, benefit with fifteen friends and colleagues, two of them previous analysands of my own. Where the work had started on a background of supervision it usually drifted back to that, with bits of self-analysis here and there. In all cases my friendship with the person was noticeably strengthened, particularly in those cases of persons older than myself with whom a certain element of mutuality tended gradually to enter into the self-analytic work.

The method I have followed has been to insist that a dream-record be kept and its text utilized in the supervisions. While I did not restrict the lines of exploration to the dreams of the supervisee, I tended to restrict my own comments to the dream itself, and particularly its formulation in terms of infantile organization of self and object relations. I tried to follow the continuity in the dream narrative from week to week once I had become familiar with the person's dream vocabulary.

Clearly these were all people who had had good analyses with which they were deeply pleased and somewhere disappointed. The disappointment always seemed to have a background in loss of idealization of one or both parents or early loss of a parent. The tenor of the dream-life struggle seemed always to centre on the attempt to re-establish some lost admiration or trust, particularly trust in the parent's (or analyst's) tolerance of the person's deviation from expectations expressed or assumed. In all those who were over seventy, some six in number, this problem had taken on urgency in relation to the apprehension of their own death. It constituted a wish to repair a primal relationship as a personal preparation. Of the fifteen people involved in this experience, in only one did I eventually feel doubtful of its value, largely because the previous analyses were less than satisfactory.

I am inclined to feel that all these friends and colleagues were still suffering the analytic illness from which they had failed to recover because of inadequate mutual experience with their analysts of the weaning process. The average length of the intensive supervision of self analysis was about two years. But what I learned from it has greatly strengthened my conviction that where an analysis has set growth in motion once again, this growth goes on in the quiet chrysalis of dream-life.

Selected Bibliography

Bion, Wilfred
Learning from Experience. Heinemann, 1962
The Elements of Psycho-analysis. Heinemann, 1963
Transformations. Heinemann, 1965
Attention and Interpretation. Tavistock Publications, 1970
A Memoir of the Future:
   The Dream. Imago Editora, Brazil, 1973
   The Past Presented. Imago Editora, Brazil, 1975
   The Dawn of Oblivion. Clunie Press, Perthshire, 1978

Cassirer, E
The Philosophy of Symbolic Forms. Berlin, 1925

Freud, S
The Interpretation of Dreams. S.E. IV and V
Mourning and Melancholia. S.E. XIV
Three Essays on Sexuality. S.E. VII
Splitting of the Ego in the Service of Defence. S.E. XXIII
On Narcissism. S.E. XIV
The Ego and the Id. S.E. XIX
Studies in Hysteria. S.E. II
The Two Principles of Mental Functioning. S.E. XII
Project for a Scientific Psychology. Basic Books, 1954
Analysis Terminable and Interminable. S.E. XXIII
A Child is being Beaten. S.E. XVII

Klein, Melanie
Envy and Gratitude. Hogarth Press, 1975 (1976)
Notes on some Schizoid Mechanisms. Hogarth Press,
   1975 (1946)
Narrative of a Child Analysis. Hogarth Press, 1980 (1951)
Psychoanalysis of Children. Hogarth Press, 1980 (1932)

Langer, Susanne
Philosophy in a New Key. O.U.P., 1951

Meltzer, Donald
The Kleinian Development. Clunie Press, 1978
The Psycho-Analytical Process. Heinemann, 1967

Meltzer, Donald et al.
Explorations in Autism. Clunie Press, 1975

Russell, Bertrand
An Enquiry into Meaning and Truth. Allen and Unwin, 1940

Sharpe, Ella
Dream Analysis. Hogarth Press, 1937

Wittgenstein, Ludwig
Tractatus. Kegan Paul, 1922
Philosophic Investigations. Blackwell, 1958

Index

DONALD MELTZER was educated at Yale and New York University College of Medicine, trained in adult and child psychiatry at Washington University in St. Louis. He came to England in 1954 to complete his psycho-analytical formation with Melanie Klein. He has worked mainly in close collaboration with Wilfred Bion, Roger Money-Kyrle and Esther Bick, teaching at the Tavistock Clinic and the Institute of Psycho-analysis where he was, until recently, a training analyst. With his wife, Martha Harris, he has taught extensively in Italy, France, Spain, Norway and South America since 1970, contributing a significant force for the revival of child analysis. His books, *The Pyscho-analytical Process, Sexual States of Mind, Explorations in Autism* and *The Kleinian Development*, have been widely translated.

THE ROLAND HARRIS EDUCATIONAL TRUST, founded as a Registered Charity in 1973, is dedicated to supporting training, therapy and research in the field of child analysis, while also being engaged in publishing (The Clunie Press).